T0147784

BEYOND THE MUSIC

Robert Taylor

Order this book online at www.trafford.com
or email orders@trafford.com

Most Trafford titles are also available at major online book retailers.

© Copyright 2011 Robert Taylor.
All rights reserved. No part of this publication may be reproduced, stored in a retrieval
system, or transmitted, in any form or by any means, electronic, mechanical, photocopying,
recording, or otherwise, without the written prior permission of the author.

Printed in the United States of America.

ISBN: 978-1-4269-6108-3 (sc)

Trafford rev. 03/28/2011

 www.trafford.com

North America & international
toll-free: 1 888 232 4444 (USA & Canada)
phone: 250 383 6864 ♦ fax: 812 355 4082

Table of Contents

Beyond The Music

I have friends in overalls whose friendship
I would not swap for the favor of the Kings of this world

Thomas Edison

This book is dedicated to the many friends and followers, who have given us so much encouragement over the years. Since our very first performance in front of a live audience, we have been blessed with the finest people we could ever ask for. Some of these friends are no longer with us but are often remembered. There are too many to mention at this point but several will come to print later on. I am sure each of you will know you have touched our hearts, and on behalf of the Last Chance Band I thank you.

The title of this book reflects my thoughts on music and the many connections that have deeply affected our lives. Music is more than just a sound. Music can take you on journeys of the mind. It may be just a few notes, or your favorite Jig or Reel but the sound will often take you to a world all of your own. It is a driving force. It has great healing powers. It can, and will, change your life. It has greatly influenced the lives of each member of our group. We also hope it has influenced our loyal followers. Most of the people who take time to read on will soon realize, that you too are a very integral part of our circle of friends. You are all part of our lives, "Beyond The Music."

The many gatherings, the joy, the new friends, the dancing, the comradery, and of course all the great food we have consumed. I am sure we will all cherish the memories in the years ahead. The music has been the common thread that brought us together, but the total fabric includes the fun we have had because of our music. We have gone beyond many times and have all had great experiences As you journey through this book, you will be reminded of a story or two, that perhaps you were a part of. I hope your journey will be a pleasant one and you too will be blessed with a lot of fond memories

1

"Touch us O God, through the ministry of melody. Be with us through the sounds and senses of song and wordless wonder which fills our souls with heaven. You are the Spirit which teaches our feet to dance and causes our hearts to overflow, that in so we might be absorbed the mystery and magic of music"

Cover Photo

The photo was taken at a 50th Anniversary Dance in June 2008. Note the Golden Ties. This was the last Dance we played with our good friend, Keith MacLennan.

Chapter One: The Beginning

It was Monday August 15th 1994. A large group of Musicians had gathered at the Ferry Terminal in Dartmouth Nova Scotia, for the arrival of the Queen. She was on her way from Halifax via the ferry and we were there to play for her. You can surely understand my excitement as I could just barely get through Twinkle, Twinkle Little Star on the Violin.

The group I belonged to at that time, the Metro Fiddlers, had been asked to play and there we were in our bright red shirts and white ties. Since we were early and I think the Queen was fashionably late, we had time to get prepared. I had a few minutes to get the last few notes of Twinkle, Twinkle. I joke of course. We played some serious stuff.

Our leader at that time was Ron Noiles, A good leader, but very traditional. He was prone to playing tunes that we had heard many times before. Please do not get me wrong, he was, and still is a good leader. In the short time I had played in his group I realized I needed to find a better way to practice. It was during this waiting time that a few of us gathered together to discuss our future in music.

Now we all know there are things that happen, that we can not explain. We do not know the reasons, just the outcome. This is certainly one of them. The group that gathered that day, Herman MacKeen, Keith MacLennan, Doug Morash, Ron Dares, and yours truly, came together for some special reason. It is not known how this particular group got together on that given day, but none of us were ever sorry. Vivian Taylor became part of that group, but was working that day. As we stood in the warm August sun, we talked about many topics but settled on music. We very quickly decided we would be able to learn much faster if we formed a smaller group. This was not a poor reflection on the group we were with, as a matter of fact we stayed with the larger group for a few years after that. It was on that August day we formed a new group and started a new direction. We had to have a name. It hit us very quickly when Herman announced that this would probably be our last chance. Thus the Last Chance Band began .

In the early days we were the original six. We decided to get together every Thursday night. We would take turns hosting our group. We first decided to go to one another's houses each week to practice for a couple of hours, have a coffee and then go home.

The coffee soon grew into a full blown lunch, and sometimes a full course meal. Now, music was our main reason for these meetings, however, I want you to know we solved many world problems as well. It was never our aim to be the best at what we did. We just wanted to have fun, and provide a lot of good entertainment for others.

3

Right away we set ourselves to the task of learning new tunes, and found ourselves very comfortable with our new group. We soon got the urge to play for some dancers, and very quickly began our plan. We hired a hall and called almost every one we knew and begged them to come hear us. That was the beginning of a great group.

It was at this first dance in St. John's Hall, in Dartmouth, that we began to meet our new circle of friends. I think the attendance that night was 39. We continued holding these dances once a month and in fact celebrated our thirteenth anniversary in May 2008

Shortly after our first dance, Nick Nicholson, and Al MacVicar joined us. Our number was then eight, and remained that way until the passing of our good friend Herman, on December 25th 2007. In July of 2008 we lost Keith MacLennon. Now our number is six, and our dear friends will long be remembered. We have been asked by a few, from time to time if they could join but not until quite recently did we consider anyone else. We did in fact invite Budd Gavel to join us early in 2009. Budd plays the violin and also a very good piano accordion. The accordion is a very nice addition to our regular music. Linda Rix, a very capable bass player is also a part time member now, and welcome to play with us whenever she is available.

When we first started, our plan was simple. Learn as many new tunes as possible. Keep them simple, and above all, learn to play good dance music. This is one area where many bands fail. Playing what they want, the way they want, and not playing what the dancers want to hear. If we have had a measure of success it has been the fact we cater to our dancers

At this point I want to make something perfectly clear. We have never considered ourselves better than any other groups, playing now, or in the past. Quite simply, we want to give our friends the best dancing music possible.

On most of these early dances one of our best friends, Stan Gray would come in through the hall door dancing all the way. Stan left us a few years ago, but we can still see him dance. He was an inspiration to us all as he always praised our music. He was a great fiddler as well and would play for us on occasion. John Warner was another friend who came to most of our dances. He carried a small tape recorder and recorded all of our tunes. We called him Big John. He has left us as well but to us he will always be there doing his special slow dance.

After Nick and Al joined our group, we started to play for other dances. We started to play in Upper Musquodoboit, and are still playing there the first Saturday of each month. We also played for a couple of years at Porters Lake. We found our schedule quite busy and reluctantly gave up the Porters Lake dance. We have played from one end of mainland Nova Scotia. To the other. We have played for many Anniversaries and Birthdays. Homes for special care are on our list and we play for three, on a regular basis.

Traveling to and from these events is quite often just as much fun as playing music. There are always many laughs, and each of us take our turn at being on the receiving end. It is also another good opportunity to solve more world problems.

I have always been affectionately known as The Boss. I have never quite figured it out, but, as long as I do what I am told, I think everything will be fine. On a more serious side, they look to me as their leader and I feel grateful for the support. We have always had a lot of two- way communication, and everyone is part of the decision-making process.

Figure 1 Rob Taylor and Stan Gray enjoying a laugh in Pictou County.

We play music together, and we are all best friends. As the book unfolds you will find we all play

5

a different role in   the group and we all have different personalities. If I were tasked with the job of choosing another group, I know I would never be able to equal this one.

Music has opened up a new world for us. It has enhanced each of our lives and I hope we can continue to enhance the lives of others. As we move on we meet more new friends, but unfortunately we lose others who have gone to a better place. Each one we lose takes a part of us with them. As each year goes by we are saddened by the passing of more friends. We are, however, blessed with the birth of young ones in our circle. Sometimes we get to see our children dancing to our music and we all hope they will remember, and carry on the tradition

My fiddle playing came about quite late in my life. I was forty five when I had my first lesson. I did not realize at that time what a major turn, in my path of life, was before me. Prior to this my only encounter was a rare occasion when I managed to pick up my father's fiddle. I think I was about six years old and I was alone with the instrument. I was not very successful and soon found other interests. It was not until later years that I heard my father remark, " The first of my family who learns to play this violin shall have it for their own" I felt sad, for not one of his eight children knew how to play. There was an exception, and it was a stretch. My oldest brother Stewart had tried to play long before I had made my first attempt. He learned to play one tune that still stands out in my mind. He soon left home to join the navy and later began to play guitar. Years later I decided I would like to give it a try. I started lessons in Dartmouth, with Bill Guest. Work commitments in Ottawa took me away from these lessons, but I do thank Bill for setting me out on the right track.
  I will be the first to admit I did not progress at a rapid pace, but I can't get over the joy of trying to improve. I can read music but I use it as a last resort. There is a never-ending debate about the pros and cons of being able to read music. Whatever works for you is right. This book is not about how good we play, it is about how good we make others feel.

Our good friend, Herman MacKeen used to quote a phrase to us, "Music is too important to be left to the professionals, There is an intrinsic value in doing something you are not the best at."

I have always tried to judge my progress by how I felt I was doing. When my friends encourage me I feel great but the inner feelings are still my best guideline. Too many people set themselves up for failure because they try too hard to be number one. My advice to anyone starting out would be, play the very best you can each time you get the opportunity. Forget about being better than others. Be yourself, develop your own style and enjoy the journey.

My journey has been a tremendous one. Some of the finest people I know , I met through music. I am not a great fiddler, nor do I expect to become one anytime soon. On a scale of 1-10 I would probably come in at a 4 or 5. If I have a strong point, and I say if, it would be my experience in working with people. Quite often the person who makes the sale, is far more important than the product they are selling. When we started our band we were all quite willing to inter-act with our audience. We kept this up and I am sure that has contributed to our success more than our music.

I have a friend who is a United Church Minister. His messages always hits the mark, however it is his presentation that makes it all stick. I hope we have done just that. Everywhere we go we get great comments, and I am sure it is because of two things, the message, and the presentation.

We have always been a team. Everyone of us knows we each contribute our share. There is nothing worse than one who insists they have to be the main performer. You know what I mean. The person who plays louder, faster, longer, and the ones who will not listen to the others in their group. We do not have anyone like that and I can assure you we never will.

My personal thoughts are very clear on our playing. Keep it simple. As long as I can I will keep going and providing people with basic dance music. When we play for any dance, we have a pattern that

7

we follow. We usually start out with, two waltzes, a fox trot or two, and then a reel. We will follow this cycle over and over, with little change. There are a few basics I have learned. I have mentioned, that you have to give your dancers what they want. Keeping a close eye on the people will give you a clear indication of how you are doing.

We never play two reels together, as much as we may like to do so. To dance a Hop Polka is a wonderful experience, but two in a row can tire you out. I have seen the results of this. When people get too tired they stop dancing, some for long periods of time. I know of one fiddler who has not learned that yet. He will play two or three reels in a row, and still can't figure out why the people stop dancing. It is all about giving the people what they want.

Another thing we do is try to remember the tunes people like best. We have a long list of tunes we play, and we are constantly adding to this list. But it is very important to listen to your requests. We take this one step further and play some of the crowd favorites before they get a chance to ask for them. Let me give you an example. When you go out and buy a new CD, you will find there are perhaps five or six tunes you really like. The rest are just so-so. Well this is a normal reaction, however, not everyone would pick the same tunes as you. That is why it is so important to keep an open mind. When someone asks you to play a certain tune, it is just the same as it is when they order food at a restaurant. If you don't oblige them they may not return.

Sometimes we play tunes and someone on stage will groan and say not that one again. Well if the dancers ask for it you had better play it. It is not rocket science, it is common sense. We want our friends to leave our dances with the urge to come back soon.

We are losing our style of music. Our new fiddlers are so far advanced in terms of ability and knowledge, however it is harder and harder now to find the good old sweet simple music we grew up with. Our group has been very fortunate in the fact we have great accompaniment. Vivian Taylor on keyboard does not have to take a back seat to anyone. Nick Nicholson, on guitar and bass, the same. Keith MacLennon, who we just lost to a band much higher up, was the best I ever heard on the banjo. Al McVicar who can play just about anything, and has the best ear for chords, tends to keep things simple. The beat is where it is at. Take all the great fiddlers you know and get them together. The ones with the beat get the applause.

Several times when I have had the opportunity to listen to other good fiddlers, I was amazed at the ability they had, only to hear later that our group could not be beat when it came to dance music. This is a wonderful feeling to a group that started out in a kitchen just to have some fun.

Each of us feel this pride and realize there is a place for us. The sad part for us is the aging factor. At our dances and others throughout the country, our population is aging, and the younger people do not dance nearly as much. I wish there were some magic we could use to entice the younger people to join in. They are sure to have fun.

The Fly Story

Our playing has taken us on many journeys across the country. Many little side events stick in my mind. One I will tell you about now is the one called, <u>The Fly.</u> We were invited to play in a variety concert in Upper Nine Mile River. This was in the heart of winter, sometime in the late nineties and the night was very cold, I remember driving there that night and wondering why we decided to go when it would have been so easy to stay home out of the cold.

It was however a real good evening, and we were glad the kind people at the fire hall had asked us to join them. When our turn came to play we were like children at their first Christmas Concert. Excited and nervous .

During the first tune we played, I happened to see a huge fly in the center of the hall. It was approaching the stage in a zig-zag fashion, wondering aimlessly towards us. I looked over at Ron Dares who was to my far right. He had his eye on this same fly and like me was wondering why a fly would be out in the cold February air. We both watched in awe as it prepared to land. Right on the tip of Herman's nose. We all knew we were in for some antics as Herman would soon fix that fly. The big fly made a perfect landing and decided to stay there until the tune was over

9

Now I want you to know , that at this point in time everyone in the hall knew the fly had landed. Herman's performance in trying to remove the fly was better than any tune we could have played. He bent his nose in several different directions to move the fly but nothing worked. He even crossed his eyes, but the fly held his ground. This was a real test for all of us to keep our composure, especially Herman. Many times later Herman would tell us he still had the scars where the fly had planted all of his feet on his nose.

These are the moments that will always be so very dear to us. The laughs, the people we meet, the ability to reach out to people with our music and the little side events that are such a bonus.

The Sticking Table

There is another event that included Keith, Herman, and myself. We were on our way to Florida, I think it was the spring of 1994. Keith was going down for a couple of weeks and asked us to join him. It was a trip I will never forget, and only now do I realize how important it was to me, as they are both gone.

We were on our third day of driving and arriving in Florida late in the afternoon. We had just crossed the Florida State line and Keith decide to stop for a bite to eat. As we approached this little town, he pulled in to a small restaurant. He headed directly towards the washrooms as Herman and I went to find a table. Now this was not the best place in the state of Florida, but we were hungry. As I picked up the menu and placed my arms on the table I realized

something was wrong. I looked at Herman and found he was having the same problem. Our arms were stuck to the table. In a few moments Keith came along and told us he was no longer hungry, and we should not visit the restrooms. We departed the restaurant and the small town. Herman stated that if the whole State of Florida was like that he was game for turning around and heading home right away. We would laugh later, as we soon realized the State of Florida was a wonderful place to visit.

10

Marking My Doughnuts

During a later trip to Florida, Keith, Herman, Doug, and myself were traveling together. As a normal practice we would shop for everything we needed, and then split the cost. This worked out quite well except there were times that Herman would balk, especially if it was something he did not like. One of his concerns was the amount of doughnuts we were eating. He felt we should cut back because he could not eat them as fast as we could.

One evening we had just came back from the market and of course we had purchased a dozen of the finest. We were putting our things away and I just happened to look towards Herman. He had a doughnut in his hand. He took one bite out of it and put it back in the bag. He repeated this exercise two more times. I asked him what he was doing and he said. "I am marking my doughnuts."
You can rest assured we did not eat any of his doughnuts after that.

Traditions of the Fiddle

The views I express here, and elsewhere in this book, are purely my own and I do not expect everyone will agree. The traditional Down-East fiddle music is rapidly changing. We are losing our culture, and many people don't seem to realize this. In this Province of Nova Scotia, we probably have more people playing the fiddle than ever before, yet we are losing our old style. How are we losing this culture and what can we do?

In the early years that I remember, every community had at least one good fiddler. Each of these fiddlers would have their own unique style. When you heard them you would know right away, without looking, who was playing. When these fiddlers leave us, we lose part of our heritage.

I feel quite confident that we have better teachers here than we ever had, but perhaps we are too rigid in our training. One person told me we were cloning our students. We are teaching them on such a high level, and pushing them to do everything exactly right, yet we don't allow them to be unique players. One of the finest examples I can think of would be our fiddle contests. The contestants train hard, some under the watchful eye of their teacher, who has taught them all they can about proper playing. They enter the contest and play as best they can, but are they ever judged by their uniqueness? Only by the audience and in most contests, that does not count. Please don't think I am against fiddle contests, I have attended more than most. I just think contestants should play for the audience and not the Judges.

When we speak we all have a voice unlike any other. When we play we should also have a sound unlike any other. I don't think our judging style gives enough credit to the actual entertainment value, as our audience does.

I will always remember a story that was told to me by a local fiddle teacher. He had taught this young lady for about four years. She went off to college and he did not see her for a few years. One evening he was at a local concert and heard her play. After the show she came out to him and asked how she was doing. He said just fine except for one major thing, you sound just like your teacher. He explained to her that she had the ability to play from her heart the way she wanted to and in order to improve she would have to do just that.

The world is shrinking and we can get music from anywhere, so we experiment. We play many more tunes and some, much more difficult than our ancestors did, but we do not play the good old traditional tunes that were the very heart of our communities.

Most of our well trained fiddlers might fall flat on their face playing at a dance. Not because they are not good enough, but because they are so bound by their own perfection that they don't keep in tune with the audience.

Times change and so do the people, but I would love to have the power to keep our traditional music and encourage the younger people to dance. When I was in my teens, I loved to go to the local dances. Dancing was a real chore for me, and I walked on a lot of toes, but it was a place to gather and have a lot of fun.

In those days the dances were held on many occasions, and quite often in homes in the community. There would be a local fiddler or two and a guitar. The better dances had piano and banjo as well. One place I attended quite often was in Elderbank, Nova Scotia. They had a real dance hall, and I think it was called the Keddy and Innes Hall. It was not elaborate, but there was always a crowd. There was never an open bar, but there was always a sip or two to be had by those who wished to take part. Smoking was rampant in those days and by ten o'clock at night the hall would be a cloud of smoke. On most nights there would be a fight or two, but I was never one for that. The music kept going and the dancers did too.

It was at one of these dances that I had my first waltz quadrille. I had gone there with my brother Mac. He was on leave from the air force, and wanted to go. He said he heard there was a family of girls from another community going and he wanted to get to know one of them. Now he was no Fred Astaire and besides he was a little bashful, so I do not remember if he danced at all. However I did get up the nerve to ask a young lady to show me the Waltz Quadrille.

We got through the set and I was a very happy camper even though I probably made a fool of myself. It was not until after this dance that I found out the girl I danced with was the main reason my brother had gone. Needless to say I had a quiet ride home and I don't think he ever invited me again. I often wonder if the poor girl had bruises on her toes the next day. Some day I will get up enough nerve to ask her. A very talented fiddler, Kirk Logan played there for several years.

Later on we would all gather in Upper Musquodoboit, at the community hall for the Saturday night dances. Mel McPhee and his band played there every Saturday evening for seven years, in the late 50's and early 60's (Mel still plays for various functions in the area). As a point of interest, we had the good fortune to meet Mel on a recent occasion in Truro. We were playing for a 50th wedding anniversary at the Legion. Percy and Donna Cox were the people celebrating. They had met at one of the dances in Upper Musquodoboit, where Mel played. They invited him to come back and play for them, over fifty years later. He still has the beat.

It was not until my family had grown, that we started going to dances again. It was also after we formed our group and started playing at these events. I was determined to learn to dance, especially the hop polka. I finally mastered it, with the excellent teaching of a couple of good friends, Karen Edwards and Audrey Rourke. I love it.

It is very pleasing to know that in this area, we could attend at least two, or three dances a week. All of which would provide the good old traditional music of our time. As I mentioned before, the group of this era are aging and we can't seem to get the younger people out. Perhaps we should start a school just for that purpose.

The Old Garage. I am going to digress for a moment, as I feel it is necessary for me to tell you a little more about my father. He was a man far beyond his time, and had a wisdom that always amazed me. There was never a job he could not do. That, I suppose was one of the reasons he played the fiddle. I did not get to hear him play more than a half dozen times in our period together, but when I did, he seemed to play and laugh at the same time.

The fiddle he had for many years, was one he acquired in payment for a late gasoline bill. It was in his garage that this transaction took place. A few years before this he had built a new garage and house in Upper Musquodoboit. He would later lose both due to the depression in the late nineteen-twenties. This was before my time, but I would later learn of his hardship during this period from my older siblings.

This very violin became the reason for my wanting to learn to play. The old garage was later renovated and we now play for dances there once a month. Every time I enter the building I get a sense that he is there laughing at me playing. As a matter of fact several people have laughed at my playing. I remember one evening we were playing in Dartmouth, Nova Scotia. A lady danced past us and said to Herman, "can't you smile?" His reply was " which do you want me to do, play or smile? I can't do both at the same time".

Back to my father. As I mentioned, I did not get much chance to hear him play, as he always needed a lot of coaxing to get started. He was a born entertainer however, with his great stories and his quick wit I think I could find an old metal pie plate at my brother Dennis's that dad used to grab, when he heard music he liked. He would bang this plate on his knees, elbows, and his head, in time to the music.

All this time he would be smiling that devilish smile of his. He was also very good at playing the handsaw. This is truly an art you don't see very often. He had great success with it and claimed you had to have a very good saw to make good music. I guess this follows true with any type of musical instrument.

My Father's brothers, and sisters were all quite musical and when they got together in my grandparents house in Wittenburg, Nova Scotia, They would surely make some noise. A sip or two of the finest brew and they were usually away to the races. Now my grandmother did not allow spirits of an alcoholic nature in the house, so the large spring down over the hill became a very popular spot. It is still there and it would not surprise me if one were to find a bottle or two, (empty of course) near the famous old spring.

15

When we were kids we would go there with our parents, and would meet other relatives for an afternoon of excitement. After a short time, you would see a group of children playing just about anywhere on the property. The men however could be found, you guessed it, down by the spring. The ladies of course would be in the parlor.

My father lived a life of hard work, with little pay. This was normal for his time, but he was not your normal person. This could be the topic of another book. To me, he was the smartest man I ever met. He could fix anything, grow anything, build anything, bake anything, and make you feel good. He was a man who never complained. If he did, I never heard him do so. He provided for his family as best he could. For many years, this was a struggle as we lost our mother when I was six years old. I am sure during these years he had many dreams and wished for better times.

He was a buddy to me and took me on several memorable fishing trips. He passed away at the age of eighty three. I will always remember the last few words I heard him say. It was in the hospital and the nurses were making him as comfortable as they could. They asked him what he wanted for breakfast. He said, " All I want is a bowl of oatmeal porridge with lots of brown sugar." He passed away that night before he got his porridge.

I have often thought of the lesson I learned from him that night. In his life he helped many people and made many laugh with his stories. He lived in difficult times and perhaps one would think he missed a lot in life, but his final wish, was for a simple bowl of porridge. I owe a lot to my father, and playing the fiddle is one of things I do to help pay my debt.

The Boys in the Trees

While this story has no real connection to music, it does have a humorous tale and well worth relating. For a short time in the Spring, when the sap is running in the trees, they become very supple. One of these trees is a Juniper. In my community there were lots of them in an area we frequented, as young boys in the country. We would find a tree that had a trunk about three inches in diameter. Climbing this tree was the first objective. You see, if we could get quite close to the top, the tree would bend. In so doing it would easily bend so far we would actually touch our feet on the ground, let go of the tree and watch it spring back in place. We would do this for great periods of time. Sometimes we would find bigger trees and two boys would climb up the same tree. This was more fun because the bigger trees were naturally taller and we got a bigger thrill.

Now around this time of year, I think it would have been the Easter break, we would always be blessed with a visit from a city boy, who knew everything there was to know. Not really, he just thought he did. He had an uncle who lived in the area, and his parents sent him to the country for an education. Being good country boys we did not have much time for this overdressed city boy. Now it was on one of our tree climbing capers, that he showed on the scene with his mouth in high gear. We asked him if he ever climbed one of these junlper trees. He replied that he had climbed much bigger ones in the city, and did not think this would be much fun.

We used our best persuasive tactics to get him to try one along with us. It worked. He agreed to give it a try. We found a good tall tree about six inches in diameter. There were three of us, besides the city slicker. I believe they were, Elliott Whitman, Ronald Decker and myself. We gave him a few instructions on the ground before we started the climb. The most important was to hang on to the tree as it started to bend towards the ground. Now you have to try and visualize this event. The tree which is at least twenty five feet high, is starting to bend towards the earth with four boys hanging on to it. As we are slowly getting closer to the ground we warn him again. Don't let go.

As the first boy touches the ground, the country boys all let go. The tree now whips back up with the city boy still hanging on. Because of the speed it was traveling it went past the original up-right position and toward the opposite position. He looked like a flag flying in the wind. After two or three more swings the tree came to rest. He came down that tree like a monkey, and told us he thought his uncle needed him at home.

17

He never bothered us for the rest of his visit. We never intended to harm him in any way, and we didn't. We just wanted to show him that he still had a few things to learn, especially if he wanted to survive in the country. Perhaps if I had been practicing my violin at this time instead of teaching the city boy, I would be a much better player today.

May you live every day of your life
Jonathan Swift

Figure 2 My Father with my three Sons Corey, Kendall and Joe, about 1970.

Chapter Two: Vivians Story.
Vivian Georgena Dean, (Taylor) Born February 27th 1939 in Chaplin, near Dean Settlement.

We cherish our friends not for their ability to amuse us, but for ours to amuse them.   Evelyn Waugh.

Figure 1 Vivian at her favorite spot.

Vivian, the only female in our group was born in Dean Settlement. High on the hills of that area, of Halifax County. If we were pressed to select the person that has been the most valued member of our group, she would win hands down. Without any doubt she has been the center of the group. Her talent for basic music, is a true gift. She is known for her keyboard playing, but she could have excelled at any instrument if she had decided to go that route.

Vivian has never been one to brag about her ability, in fact she is probably a little too quiet about her capabilities. She has remarkable timing skills, great ear for music, and her ability to learn so fast. This is so very important when playing good dance music. The major reason for our modest success has been our timing. Vivian has always been on the money when we play.

Quite often we tend to forget our back-up and concentrate on the fiddles when we play. The best music is always created when every instrument can be heard.

In her own words. "My first musical interests came when I was three or four years old. At my grandmother MacKays there was a Melodian, and a pump organ at aunt Eileens. She taught me one little song to chord to. From then on when I saw black and white keys, I had to touch.

The Melodian is in my living room thanks to my mother's twin sisters, Lois and Lila. They were the owners of the instrument.

My grammy Dean had an organ they used for hymn sings. They always tried to keep me out of the parlor but I would slip in and play a few notes. My uncle Lester played guitar, and my uncle Win Dean played the fiddle for dances in the Dean School House. They played by the light of an oil lantern, Ha! I had a nap in the afternoon so I could go to the dance in the evening to sit by the music.

I would also babysit six to eight children, for one family near by. It was a good opportunity to play the guitar they had. I tuned it, and played it with a kitchen knife, as a steel guitar. My mother had a fiddle that belonged to her brother. She kept it behind the parlor couch, just in case someone might drop in. When they did, it could be for a birthday party, a house party, or perhaps just a few tunes.

As a teenager she saved her babysitting money and purchased her very own Piano, (which she still Plays). From that day on she became very dedicated to the Piano, and learned very quickly. For several years during marriage and raising children, she gave up music. She would, however play for fiddlers from time to time, (one of them being Kirk Logan and another, Mel McPhee,) but it was not until recent years that she began to play more frequently.

It must be difficult, being the only female in our group, however she mentions it only on rare occasions. There are times when we have ladies playing with us but not on a regular basis. Ron Dares has often referred to her as our Den Mother. We have also been referred to as Snow White and the Seven Dwarfs. (Perhaps one day we will name them).

Vivian has never taken any formal training other than basic music lessons in high school. During this period she was asked to accompany all the singing classes at the annual music festival, on the piano. She does have a good understanding of music. Her main strength is her ear for music. She did take violin lessons from Ron Noiles for two or three years and could do very well if she had time to play more. Being a piano player for our group keeps her busy.

Like the rest of the group she gives us reason to laugh, at her expense, from time to time. One of these times was at The American Legion, in Zepher Hills Florida. We were playing for a group one evening. There was an old beat up piano. Actually when I think of it, the whole place was beat up. We were having a lot of fun playing and a few were dancing. Sometime close to the end, the old chair she was seated on decided, it had enough, and collapsed. The piano stopped and we all looked her way. She was on the floor. Once we found out she was ok, we all had a good laugh. We still do.

Laughter has played a very important role in our success. I want to elaborate on that term, success. There are many levels of success. Ours is measured by the amount of enjoyment we give to others, and the amount of fun we have doing it. If we make people happy and we have fun, we must be doing something right. It reminds me of a friend I used to know. He was a working buddy of mine in Ottawa Ontario. He spoke English but his first language was French.

We were in a discussion about doing our best. He would later use his version, saying, "We do the best we are" We laughed with him about this, but it always remained with me. I think it is a fitting way to describe the Last Chance Band. We do the best we are. You see, as long as we can, we will play, enjoy, and make others happy.

On a recent occasion we were playing at a Home for special Care and when the time came for us to leave, a lady who had been there for almost two hours, said to us, "you folks have given me the best moments I have had in a very long time". She was not concerned about the few mistakes we may have made, she was happy with the results of our playing. Moments like these make our time volunteered worth any small amount of effort on our part.

A few years ago Vivian had a serious bout with Colitis. She was very sick for several months. She missed a lot of our playing events and I think this was one of her worst setbacks. No matter how tired she gets, when someone mentions music she finds new life.

Losing our banjo player was very hard on all of us but I think it was especially hard on her as they looked to each other for help on Chords, while playing.

The pictures below show Viv at her piano on the left and playing for a concert in upper Musquodoboit on the right. Also another of her and her sister Nina, and brother Freeman

Figure 2 Charman Fraser dancing while Vivian played. This was at a Concert in Upper Musquodoboit.

Figure 3 Vivian at her piano. She still has it.

Figure 4 Nina, Freeman, and Vivian.

Chapter Three Herman's Story.

The truest expression of a people is in its dance and its music
Bodies never lie   Agnes de Mille.

Meet Herman MacKeen, Perhaps small in stature, but a man with a Big heart. Born April 26 1927. It would take more than one book to describe the magnitude of this man. He tells me being a country boy was not easy. He had to walk two miles to School, and two miles back and it was up hill both ways.

The picture on the left shows him at a very early age, playing a fiddle. He was cute then, and still is. He was one of the original six in our group and has always given us lots of laughs, as well as many sweet notes on several instruments.

Herman spent a lot of his working years as a Mechanic, Teacher, and School Bus Driver. He also tried his hand at farming in Pictou County. He is always a great source of valuable information. He can also provide you with a lot of worthless information, but funny. He has a flair for story telling.

I remember one story he told about his trips to Antigonish. He lived in the small community of Aspen, several miles from Antigonish. His father would often take him on his business trips to town. Being a very busy man, Herman's father would always wait for a rainy day to go to town. Herman said he was sixteen before he realized it did not rain every day in Antigonish.

This brings to mind a story about my childhood years, some of which were spent in Sunnybrae Pictou County. I used to spend a few weeks there in the summer with my great Aunt. The old house was very hot and sleep was very difficult most nights. One day I strolled into my uncle Jim's Shed to spend some time. During a very pleasant look around I saw a pair of Skis. I was very young then and could not understand why anyone would want skis in such a warm place. It was a few years before I learned they did indeed have lots of snow in the winter.

Back to Herman. He started playing Fiddle at a young age, however, like a lot of people, raising a family came first. He joined the Sherbrooke Oldtimers Fiddle Club several years before I met him. He still plays some of those old tunes he learned then.

Some of my favorite times with Herman were our trips to Florida. We made four trips. Three by car, and one he flew down with three other guys. They will remain nameless for now. On each of these occasions, laughter was abundant.

When we were driving he would always be on the move, and not necessarily in the direction the car was moving. The trip he made with Vivian and I, she once remarked he was like his own Jack Russell Terrier, bouncing from seat to seat.

One year there were four of us went together. Keith Maclennan, Doug Morash, Herman and myself. We had a great trip and were on our way back. We were driving along the outskirts of New York City. Keith was driving and Doug was the navigator. Herman and I were in the back. Herman said to me, look at the New York skyline, we may never get to see it again. Twenty minutes later we were in the middle of the George Washington Bridge. Oh yes, and did I say Doug was our navigator.

There are many stories I could tell about everyone in our group, and I will do my best in other chapters. Once when we were in Florida, as a matter of fact it was the same group. We had rented a Park Model unit for two weeks and had agreed to split the costs. We would take turns doing the Cooking. All except Keith. He would do the cleaning. Well let me say he did the cleaning. You would hardly get your rear off of the toilet seat before he was there to clean it. The seat that is.

The other three did do the meals. One afternoon we had company. Herman's Sister-in-law and Brother-in-law came for a visit. It was Herman's turn to get supper. As he was preparing his meat balls and veggie's, as well as joining us in some music, the potatoes boiled dry. He yelled out from the kitchen, what was that last tune you played? His Brother-in-law replied I think it was The little Burnt Potato. We all had a good laugh, and of course a good supper.

I mentioned before how we all worked well as a group. It could be compared to baking a Cake. In order for the finished product to come out looking good and also good to eat, one must have the proper ingredients. Herman has always been one of the main ingredients. We will call him the frosting for now.

Since the beginning of this book, our true friend Herman, has taken ill with cancer. We all wish we could stop time for a while, or even turn it back a little, but much to our dismay, we can not do this. There is not a day goes by that I don't stop for a moment and recall some of the great times we have had.. I know I speak for all of the Band and our friends when I say we pray every day that he recovers.

Playing with Herman has always been more than just the music. There is always a story or two, and of course many laughs. Yes I have said it before and I will close with this statement. Herman is and always will be the Icing on our Cake. Our band has been influenced immeasurably by his presence. That feeling, my friends will never leave us.

On Christmas day 2007 Herman left us for his place in heaven. There has been a deep feeling of sadness for all of us ,especially his family. His funeral was held in Glenelg Guysborough county December 28th. Bad weather conditions kept some of us at home that day, however we managed to make it to East Noel the following day for a Memorial service. The family asked the last chance band to play at this service. We have all played at several funerals, but for me this one was the hardest. We lost one of our best friends. The day of this service was a very snowy day and the driving was not the best. I will never forget the drive and thinking how important it was to be going there.

In times of sadness it is always wise to concentrate on the light, instead of the darkness. Herman's passing gave us a look at the dark side, but the light he gave us, will help us during the troubled times.

I have included the text of the Rev. Chuck Paterson. These are the exact words he used at Herman's Memorial Service.

<u>Celebration for the Life of Herman Ralph MacKeen</u>

I only knew Herman for a short time and I tried to think of a way to describe him that would be recognizable by everyone here. The few words that I think speak loudly of Herman would be humble, introverted and talented.

We often think of introverted people as being shy when in reality they are reflective and weigh things out. This was my impression of how Herman embraced his faith He knew the scriptures and didn't just hear the words but owned them as his compass in life.

He was humble and I never saw or heard him exemplify who he was. He was quiet and soft spoken with no need for bravado. He recognized his gifts and saw them as an opportunity to bring joy to others. His quiet smile was his acknowledgment of others talent and gifts a lesson in spirit of humility for each of us.

His wonderful talent was best exemplified by his music but that was just a part of all the gifts he had. He was a father, husband, musician, and teacher. All gifts he shared without expectations of returns. He reminds me of the passage of scripture that states, "Walk humbly and know that I am God" (paraphrased).

His love of family is something that you can share with them later but now we continue to pay tribute to his love for music. We know he is listening and we will see and feel that quiet smile of approval as only he could share.

Herman know that you are loved and that your memory will carry us all as we move forward from here in our journey to meet with you again in heavens eternal bliss. Amen.

I will never forget the sincerity in the voice of Rev. Paterson as he spoke that day. He knew Herman for a short time, but he must have been very impressed.

One year has passed since we lost our good friend. Sadness is still there, but his light will always shine on us.

Snake skins in the Haunted Fiddle.

This is a story about a Fiddle I bought from two brothers in Porters Lake several years past. After a few visits to look at this great old fiddle I was successful in buying it. I did a complete restoration on it and decided it would be added to my small collection The gentlemen who sold it to me said it had been their Father's, but had not been played for many years. They said I should also know it was Haunted. They told me when their dad would play it at night, there would always be a lady dressed in white run around outside the house. They never did find out who the lady was or why she did this, only that it always happened.

When I purchased the fiddle, I could see a reluctance in their faces, to let it go, even though we had agreed on a fair price. I assured them I would bring it back after I had finished the restoration. At this time if they wanted it back all they would have to do is pay me for my work and the instrument would be theirs. They decided all they wanted me to do was bring it back to show them, have a drink of rum with them, and play a tune for them. I did all three.

When I was repairing the fiddle I discovered two Snake skins inside the body. This was an old custom believed to help control the humidity. I carefully removed these an put them in a safe spot until the instrument was totally finished. I later placed them back in the fiddle to make sure they

Figure 3 Herman After a game of Golf.

would continue their duty.

A year or two later, my good friend Herman MacKeen convinced me the fiddle would look much better at his house than mine, so I sold it to him. A few weeks later I called him to see how the fiddle was working. He said, just fine, but you know what? I discovered it had some snake skins inside, so I took the vacuum cleaner and sucked them out! So the instrument may still be haunted, but the snake skins are gone.

This is another story that fits in with this subject. The two brothers I bought the fiddle from never had a car as far as I know. Instead they always used bicycles as their method of transportation. A few summers ago one of them went to pick up a few items for the pantry, and of course a trip to the local liquor store. It being a hot day, he decided a drop or two of the good stuff would be quite nice. While cycling along the road he seemed to swerve a bit too far and went off the road, landing deep in the Alder bushes. Just then a Police patrol car came along and saw him pulling his bike out of the bushes. The officer asked him if he had been drinking, and he replied. Just about all I could stand!

I will always treasure the time I spent with our dear friend. He was a man who exemplified the life of an honest, hard working man. I don't think anyone enjoyed our Thursday night sessions more than he did. He had a grate attitude towards playing. He may not have been a champion at his music, but he sure was a happy performer.

Chapter Four: Crazy Things we do.

Music washes away from the soul,
the dust of everyday life. Berthold Auerback

It is a good thing we were never told to be serious. From the first day we started, we have always kept things very light and easy. Even when we practice we have more of a jam session than a practice. When we go out to play, we try to provide the best possible music we can but we still keep it light. That is how we are able to keep going, and relate to all of our dancing friends.

There are times when we get to have a little extra fun, and do things that are out of the ordinary. One of those times came when we were asked to play for Herman and Hazel MacKeen's anniversary. That was a time we will never forget. It was a very hot summer night. We were playing in Lower Sackville, at the Lions Club. Herman was with us at that time but since he was celebrating his anniversary, we decided to give him a little surprise.

Figure 1 Robert Taylor, Vivian Taylor, Ron Dares, Keith MacLennon and Doug Morash. Let the games begin.

I don't know where the idea originated but we decided to dress up as women at some point during the evening, and pass ourselves off as Herman's old girl friends. Well, it all went off like clockwork. Doug Morash's wife Betty did the introductions one at a time. Vivian Taylor played the keyboard, and Bobby Watters played the violin, as we slowly walked up to the head table. We did this several minutes apart to give Betty time to give a full description of each one as they approached.

Preparation for this event gave us many opportunities for laughter. Keith MacLennan started the laughter by saying he would not have anything to do with dressing like a lady. But when the time came to do so and Betty produced a whole bag of clothes, he was the first one to pick his wardrobe.

When the night arrived and we were in the basement getting dressed the laughter was uncontrollable. It was hot and we were unaccustomed to this type of clothing. When we finally finished this chore and were ready for the grand entrance, Ron Dares decided a trip to the washroom was in order. He was not sure which he should use, male or female. That one almost did us in. I think a picture or two would be appropriate and will most likely be found somewhere in the book. The final analysis: the anniversary was a success and we all had a wonderful time.

On another occasion we were asked to play for a Wedding Reception. This was also a grand time. Basil and Betty-Anne Miller had just been married and wanted us to help with the entertainment. Being the adventurous group, we agreed to do it. We also put a different spin on the situation by dressing in some old work clothes and passing ourselves off as a few of Betty-Anne's old boy friends. Once again we acquired the help of Betty Morash to introduce us, one at a time. At this time Al McVicar, and Nick Nicholson were with us so we had seven men making fools of themselves.

I don't think there is any better way to enjoy life than to have fun with music. On this night we played well and had a lot of laughs. We met new people, and talked with many of our old friends. But perhaps most important, we helped a wonderful couple enjoy the moment and certainly warmed the hearts of many others.

As I mentioned before, we played for many dances. One of these was Porters Lake. We played there once a month for a couple of years. It was a great Hall and we enjoyed it, but we were too busy at the time and felt we should cut back. I am not sure we made the right decision, as we all missed it but when you are all seniors, there is only so much one can do. This was the only dance we played at where they had an open bar. (This had nothing to do with our decision to stop playing.) In all the nights we played there, I don't think they made enough at the bar to pay for the Bar tender.

If you are old enough, (and if you are not, you are not likely reading this book) please go back about thirty or forty years, and picture a Country Dance. You would not have an open bar. The refreshments would be hidden outside, or in a man's jacket or a lady's purse. Much of which would be consumed. There would be cigarettes in the hands of a large majority. The smoke would be as thick as black flies in the woods on a hot July day. Oh! how things have changed.

Back to Porters Lake. My point is, without the bar or cigarettes, the dances are so much better. I remember several years ago, a lady called me to ask about our dances, in St. John's Hall, Dartmouth Nova Scotia. She said, "Is there smoking allowed, and do you have a bar?" I hesitated for a moment, I had to tell her the truth, but I did not want to lose a potential dancer. This is the marketing background kicking in. When I explained to her that we did not have a bar and, smoking was out, she was very pleased. She said, " When people drink, I don't have to drink. But when people smoke, I have to smoke". That is when the term, second-hand smoke really hit home with me.

Figure 2 One of our dances in Porters Lake

As far as I know they still have dances in Porters Lake and I wish them well. It was suggested on one occasion that we were upset with the committee there and that was the reason for us leaving. That was false. We liked the people very much.

One evening we were playing there and the Bar came in handy. It was a cold winter night and the furnace was not performing very well.

Figure 3 Viv, Rob, Doug, Ron, Al, Herman, Nick, Keith. One of our last Dances together.

It was not too bad for the Dancers as they were moving enough to keep warm. We were on the small stage, which was one step above the dance floor. I was standing next to an outside wall, which appeared to have frost on it. My fingers were too cold to hit the right notes. I always miss several , but this was real bad. When we took our break, I headed for the bar. I remember Keith shouting, "I will have one of the same" None of us are what could be called serious drinkers, and a few would not touch a drop. I must say, however, a few of us were quite warm the rest of the evening and the remainder were still cold.

This brings to mind an evening without power at St. John's Hall in Dartmouth. It was New Years Eve,. I think it was in the late nineties. We had a large crowd invited to help celebrate. Not long after we started to play the power went out. It was cold that night, and we had a lot of food that had to be heated, not to mention the coffee, tea and hot cider. Panic did not hit us but it was just around the corner.

We lost our sound system and had to play a little louder. The cold seemed to add to the ambience of the evening. We had candles galore, and soon the crowd started to enjoy the moment even more. We ate by candle light and continued to enjoy the evening I remember well, the moans and groans when the power came back on. I think we lost power for about three hours. We put out the lights as soon as the power returned. We were happy to get some warmth, from the furnace, but the candles served us well for light. Everyone there formed a special bond. It will always be remembered as the night the lights went out on New Year's Eve.

Halloween night at St. John's Hall was always a lot of fun. One night we had over thirty people dressed up in costumes. There were too many to mention individually, but Basil Miller stands out as one. Basil is about six foot six and not overly fat. It was always difficult for him to disguise himself so we would not know him. He tried many things. You will see a picture of one of his costumes. He always got a huge round of applause when he entered the room. The one time he really had us wondering was the night he came with stilts. He looked so tall we thought perhaps it was someone else. Another time he came as a three legged man. Always a Jester, but a real gentleman.

I remember one of the times we were in Florida, Basil flew down with Doug, Ron and Herman. When he arrived he had a very bad cold. He was very determined to keep up with the rest, in spite of his illness. One afternoon, or late morning, we set out for Pinellas Park at St. Petes for the annual Nova Scotia picnic. It was held every February and I suppose it still is. It is a grand event and a great time to meet others from back home. While we were in the middle of a little jam session, Basil collapsed. We were sure he was a goner as the old folks would say. We were lucky as a nurse was handy and made sure he was ok. He had been so weak from the cold he just fell backwards. We left right away for the nearest clinic, and then to a small Hospital where he remained for three days.

When he came out he appeared to be much better. We took him to a place called Plant City. There they have a place that has the biggest Strawberry Shortcake you ever saw. Basil had one that day and he enjoyed every bite. From that day on we had a great time. Basil and his wife Betty-Ann have always been loyal supporters of our events, and Betty-Ann is still the honorary President of our Fan Club.

Playing the Exhibitions

We have had several opportunities to play at these events and each one has been a great experience. Our trip to Yarmouth, N.S. Was one of the best, as it was a two day event. The trip to and from was also a lot of fun as we toured along the way. We got payed enough to pay for our Motel, and put on two one hour shows. The people seemed to enjoy our style of music and welcomed us back. We never did get another invitation, however. I guess they decided there had to be better entertainment out there somewhere.

We played in Middle Musquodoboit on two occasions and we are going to another very soon. This one is an outdoor show with a small band shell. It is a lot of fun, especially for those of us who are from that area. Country folks are always closer to the earth and have more appreciation for the simple things in life. When playing there, as at any exhibition, one has to be ready for just about anything. You never know who or what you might see. The smell of livestock mixed with cotton candy, the site of a drunk wondering around trying to remember if he was going to, or coming from, the beer tent. Or perhaps a little old lady with a walker trying to wheel her way through the crowd to hear you play her favourite tune.

On one of our trips we had a gentleman come directly from the beer tent to our stage and give us a little dance. It was all good clean fun and he did not cause a problem. I must say he endured a lot of tunes, and continued to beat his steel toed boots on the floor in front of our stage. This is all part of the mix at any exhibition. It is a life style far better than some of the ones we would encounter deep in the centre of our larger cities.

Figure 4 The antics of Basil Miller playing The Fireman's Reel?

I have fond memories of those country exhibitions, when we were young. The Midway was always a treat. We would save every penny we could for months, just to go there and take the ladies for a ride on the Ferris Wheel.

I preferred the Ferris Wheel to all others, as it did not go around horizontally. I was a wimp when it came to the fast moving swing rides. I preferred to be home alone, to being sick in a crowd. I am sure there are a few who are still mad at me for not going on the Tilt-a-Whirl with them. If I had, I would still be trying to get my eyes focussed.

We have played a lot of concerts and in a few Malls over the years, but dances are our thing. People have so much fun when they dance, and the feeling seems to penetrate our bodies and make us play better.

Life for us goes far beyond the music and dance. The new friends we have met, the fun we have in our group, the trips we make, are all part of the mix. We also belong to another very important group, **The Down Home Fiddlers.** There are a lot of good people in this large group. I truly believe, when put to the test they are the best fiddle group in the area. There is also a newer group called the **Bedford Fiddlers**, which most of us belong to as well. We certainly have our opportunities, and for the most part we take advantage of them.

Our friend Basil Miller was one of the founding members of the Bedford group. He was also one of the first members of the Metro fiddlers. And last but not least, he was the first President of the Down Home Fiddlers.

When you speak of something funny or different to do, Basil and Betty-Ann are always there to help out. If you ever have an opportunity, get them to tell you about some of their camping heroics. They too have a great way of telling true stories and making them so interesting.

I guess by now you have realized just how much I appreciate the true art of story telling. I often think back to the days when we were younger, and that was our radio and television, of today.

I yearn for those days when we never locked our doors, the keys were always in my Dad's truck. People did not need an appointment to call on their friends. We stood at attention whenever we heard, O Canada. We wore our caps, only when we were outside, and the peak was always pointed straight ahead. We had total respect for our Parents, the Minister, our Teachers, the Policemen, and everybody loved a Fireman. Where have we gone wrong, and can we bring some of it back?

Perhaps with our playing and the help of so many of our good friends, we have made a change. Each time we play we try to include some of the old tunes that take us back. We play at several homes for special care, and when we do, there are certain tunes that bring the residents back to life. There are many, but one that stands out for me is, **My wild Irish Rose**. Quite often when we play this tune, you can see them come to life. Some with a little tear in their eye and others will sing like they did years ago.

We have played in many places, but I think the Milford rec hall would be considered the best place to play. The acoustics are so good, and we always have a fun crowd. We play there for benefit dances mostly, and the Braeside Home for Special Care is one of our favourites. We get the most pleasure out of giving to others, and watching the people dance.

Playing in Wentworth, Nova Scotia, has always been one of my personal favourites. There is a great hall there, and always a great crowd. We do not have our whole group there very often, but a few of us go once a month. They hold their dances on the last Sunday afternoon of each month. Charley Patriquin and his crew of volunteers put on an exceptional afternoon. They have a house band there and fiddlers come from all over to take part. The dance floor is great and what a joy to play there and look out and see over two hundred people dancing. For the fiddlers it is a chance to hone their playing skills.

When I first started playing there I was very nervous, as there were so many good fiddlers. I soon learned however that I could hold my own if I kept the music simple.

Anytime we attend a function where there are several fiddlers, there is something we should all consider. Each one is at a different playing level. This is a good thing for several reasons. If you have ten fiddlers, their ability will range from one to ten. It is not important where you place. This is not a contest. What is very important is how the dancers see, and hear you. Just think how boring it would become if every fiddler sounded the same. I know I am not the most adept fiddler in any crowd, but I have the confidence to provide good dance time music. We live in a very competitive world, however it is very wise to get out of the race, and just enjoy the trip sometimes. So what if someone is a lot better than we are, it is an incentive to play better next time.

Each time we go to Wentworth it is such joy in seeing the large crowds have so much fun. We started going to these dances about tens years ago, and I sure hope they continue. They have a wonderful facility and the people really enjoy the dancing. I have encouraged several others to join in and they have all had a great time.

Yes, we do some crazy things, but we also do good things. We love to make people happy and we give of our time whenever we can. I could not even guess the amount of hours we have given or the money we have donated. That part is not important. Making people happy and giving them a dance or two is important.

Figure 5 Last Chance band and friends at Oceanview Manor. Left to Right. Rhodes, Lorne, Gary, Budd, Paul, Doug, Al, Dianne, Rob, Nick, and Vivian.

Chapter Five: Charles Keith MacLennan

Born March 27th 1933, Millsville, Pictou County
Nova Scotia

*Nothing but heaven itself is better than a friend
who is really a friend*   Plautus

Figure 1 Keith about 2001

My first experience with the banjo and music was when I was about fourteen years old. A gentleman, Doug Campbell, finished high school and came to stay at the house to work with my father. Doug was learning to play the fiddle. My father showed me a couple of chords on the banjo and after several attempts, Doug and I managed to get together on a tune called "Whalens Breakdown". The banjo, (May Bell) purchased new by my father in 1928 from Eatons is one I still have and play a fair amount.

As time passed, I played the banjo for many dances in the Scotsburn and surrounding area. Many with Bob Watters and other members of his family. In 1954, I left home for a business course in Halifax for a year, after which I started working there and with the exception of five years in Moncton, N.B. have remained in Halifax.

Retirement time came Oct. 22/92 from CAN-MED surgical Supplies Ltd. (Now CAN-MED Health Care) and about a month later I picked up the old (May Bell) banjo once again. It had been over 30 years since I had the banjo on my knee. However, have enjoyed every moment of playing the banjo ever since. Especially with the band we started approx 13 years ago called "The Last Chance Band"

Being asked to join the other members of the band has to come first as a high point for me. We have formed a great friendship between us and I look forward to the time we spend together, practicing on Thursday evenings and playing for dances. Of course we cannot forget the stops at "Tim Hortons" on our way home from a dance either late in the evening or early in the morning.

Down-east old time music is great for the soul and helps keep us younger in mind at least. If you dance, the exercise is excellent for you. It is great for us in the band when we see a good number of dancers on the floor having a good time.

Knowing Keith has been a great experience for me and I am sure that goes for all the other band members. Keith is a very talented player. His attitude towards playing and his very accurate timing sets him apart from most others. Keith is well known for his generosity and his very positive approach to life in general. When he is playing it is not difficult to see how much pleasure he derives from the music. He is a team player all the way and we miss him dearly when he is not with us. It is no secret that if you want a good brand of down-east music, you better have a banjo. When you are dancing to a good reel, the banjo gives you that little extra snap.

Keith has always been very enthusiastic about our group and is usually the first to agree to go on our many gigs. One of his favorite lines is, "when will I pick you up?" Keith has never really acquired a nickname from us but a fitting one would be Mr. Clean. I say this very affectionately as I have a great deal of respect for this gentleman. Once you have traveled with him you would see what I mean, by the condition of his Suburban. It is always spotless. On one of our trips to Florida, we rented a Park Model unit at an RV Park. There were four of us, and he agreed to do the cleaning. (Also mentioned in another chapter).Well, I want you to know he did not let us down. The place was spotless all the time. On most occasions if we wanted to use the toilet facilities we would have to make sure he was not there cleaning the floor.

Keith also had a thing with paper towels. He went through roll after roll just trying to tidy up our vacation home. There were four guys on this trip and the other three sure got a lesson on housework.

One of my fondest memories of Keith was at his Mock Wedding. You see Keith and his wife Barb went to florida to get married. I think it was Barb's sister Dorothy who decided we should have a mock wedding for them when they got back. I was asked to be the

Figure 2 Keith in his early years.

best man. By the way, this was a total surprise to the new Bride and Groom. Barb's Sister Dorothy was the Bride's Maid, and Ralph Scott stood in as the minister. It was a great party, with plenty of laughs and great music. I remember it well, because in spite of the fact it was just a mock wedding, I felt like I was helping to support a great friend.

In a normal lifetime we meet many friends. Most of them good friends. And then there are the real good ones. I am fortunate to be able to say, Keith is one of those very good friends. He would never interfere, but if he sensed you were not up to par he would find some way to make things better.

Special Note, Today is a very sad day for all of us who knew Keith. This is July 3rd. 2008. Yesterday we lost our good friend Keith. I can not explain the empty feeling I have at this time. The sudden loss is very devastating to everyone. I will continue with this chapter after I have time to face the cold hard reality of losing our buddy.

It has been two weeks now, and slowly I realize that memories, of Keith are all we have left now. A great friend and banjo player has been taken from us. Our band has been hit with a tremendous blow but we will never forget the joy we had when he was with us. There will never be a day go by that we will not think of Keith. He was such an integral part of our band, not to mention our lives.

At this point in our lives I am not sure of the future of the Last Chance Band. I wish I could say we will be fine but at this point our path is not clear.

On Sunday September 21st 2008, we played at Middle

Stewiacke, in the afternoon. It was our second dance without Keith. Later in the day, a great fiddler and friend, (Dave Buckler) asked if he could play the banjo for us for a couple of tunes. When I heard the ring of the banjo, tears filled my eyes, and I am sure the same was true for the rest of the band. I am not sure if Dave realized just how much we appreciated him doing this for us but it will never be forgotten.

I look at my own banjo hanging on the wall and wonder if I could ever play it just enough to bring back some of the fond memories. I guess not. We will take our time and keep playing as long as we can. Every time we go on a trip to play, there will be space for Keith and Herman.

I had the good fortune to accompany Keith on a trip to the Annapolis Valley just before he died. We were both very interested in antiques. He wanted to see a banjo that was for sale, and I wanted to have a second look at an old car. We went to see the car first. It was a 1952 Chev. Two door. We talked, me into it.

Our next stop was for the Banjo. Much like the one in the picture. It was a Gibson four string. It was made in 1925. After looking at it for some time I decided he should have it so he bought it. We laughed about this all the way home. He convinced me to buy the car and I pushed him to buy the banjo. It was not much of a chore for either of us.

As we go through life we meet lot of friends. We could put them in categories, depending on how well we liked them. Keith was the friend of all   friends to me. He was the most dependable person I ever met.

Keith my friend, the sound of your banjo will always ring in our hearts. Thank you for the beautiful music and your pleasant smile as you played.

Figure 3 I think this would be, Sister Shirley, Keith, and their Dad. In later years Keith would restore this tractor and put in several parades.

Figure 4 The second Tractor was Keith's. Westville parade.

Figure 5 Two of our very good friends who have left us Herman MacKean, and Bun Webber. One can only imagine the topic of this conversation.

Chapter Six:

Ronald Edward George Dares. Born May 27th 1931
Dartmouth Nova Scotia

The more I live, the more I think that humor is the saving sense.
Jacob August Riis

Figure 1 Ron in the early days. Note the beard.

I started taking lessons at Findlay school at age nine. At twelve years I played classical violin with my Sister Corinne, who accompanied me on the Piano. We played in concerts, and Minstrel shows in Dartmouth churchs, and schools.

At age twenty three While attending Normal Collage in Truro I played in a Country and Western Band. Forty years later, The Last Chance Band was Born.

Some of my high points since we started are, The Last Chance trip to Florida, in 1996, and all the places we played, and people we met. The night we held our first dance at St. John's Hall. The trips to Possum Lodge, Parrsboro, our Golf games, and our many good laughs.

Thirteen years have gone by since we first started, and we are still making music, good friends, and lasting memories.

Ron has been a great asset to our group from day one. His ability to read music so well, has given us an opportunity to learn new tunes and expand our musical knowledge. His classical training has also helped to improve our playing, as a group.

Ron is one of our jokers. He is always telling stories, or is part of a story being told by someone else. Never one to complain. In fact he is always willing to go with the flow. (not always a good thing with this group.) Ron has always been a hit with our dancing friends, not just for his playing, but also for his prowess on the dance floor. There are many stories we could tell about Ron. Everyone of them would be nice clean stories. Speaking of clean stories

The Water Boy.

I will tell you about his duties as water boy at Possum Lodge (This is a small retreat we visit a couple of times a year, just for some R & R.) When we go, each person has domestic duties. One of Ron's duties was to supply us with water. One evening after the dinner meal Ron went down to the river with his pail for water. He bent over near the river, stood on a flat rock and filled his bucket. As he started to stand up, the rock began to move to one side and Ron went rolling into the river. Now Ron, being very careful not to waste water, held the pail up so he would not spill a drop. The only part of his body that did not get wet was one arm. You guessed it. The arm that held the bucket. We praised Ron for his efforts many times since. You see in the spring of the year, (and it was) there are, about 3000 gallons of water per minute going past the point where he got the water. For that reason it is very important not to spill any. Ron has been very good about his demotion ever since. You see now when we go, he is confined to the cabin, unless accompanied by another adult.

The Panty Hose

When we first met Ron, he was, shall we say in a period of transition. He was living alone. At that time. we were more interested in music, than things of a personal nature. There was one occasion however, that we had to wonder how alone he really was. We were having a practice at our house. I had put on quite a wood fire. Ron had decided it was time to take off his pullover sweater. As he pulled the sweater off, a pair of panty hose fell out. Now let me tell you I have never seen him move so fast as he did to try and retrieve that piece of clothing. All eyes were upon him on that night. However we never mentioned it again.

During the many trips to and from our gigs, we have had many a funny story. Ron would be the one to contribute most of the material. For some strange reason Ron and I seem to find reasons to laugh at the same things and have formed a bond in this regard. Perhaps we are both a little strange. During our travels we can usually find many reasons to laugh. Knowing Ron has been a great experience in my life. He is a great guy to have on our team. In the thirteen years I have known him I have never heard a harsh word spoken against him. He has always been a real team player. He has always been a quiet person while we are playing. It is during our off time that the devil shows.

Ron's talents are not limited to his playing ability. He is an excellent artist. I have seen, and, I am a proud owner of some of his work. (see below.) Ron has many talents but is never one to expound on them.

I have talked to him on several occasions about his Paintings and have purchased a few for gifts. He has a very large collection of scenes, that he has taken with his camera, and then paints them. The one further on is a picture of our old camp I referred to in another chapter. The original picture was taken by me when I was on a snowmobile ride to make on the fire. One of us always did this early so it would be warm when we dropped in later in the day. It was always nice to spend time there and enjoy a cup of tea. This picture now hangs on my son Kendall's living room wall.

It is a reminder of his childhood days when his Grandparents would take him there. It is just across the river from Possum Lodge. You will read more about possum lodge in another chapter. When I first met Ron I was pleasantly surprised that he painted. He had dozens of examples and I encouraged him to get them out where they could be seen. I know his wife Judy has also done the same. He is one of those people who hide's their light under a bushel.

Figure 2 Ron a few years ago.

Ron has a tremendous compassion for his friends. He keeps in touch with many of his past friends and co-workers. On many occasions when we meet he will tell us of friends he has met, and also many who have passed
away. Going to funerals is very common for Ron, because he cares deeply.

I would like to tell you another short story about Ron and the deer. When we travel to and from our gigs we are always on the lookout for deer. It is always a pleasure to see them in the field, but not on the roads. Now it is not a secret. Viv has the keen eye for deer followed by Al.

Figure 3 Ron's Painting of an Old Camp by the Musqodoboit River..

Ron has said many times, " I would just love to see deer just once before Viv does." It almost happened once, when we were on our way to, Middle Stewiacke to play for a birthday party. Just as we turned into the hall, Ron saw four deer in the back field. He was so excited he could not get the words out before Viv saw them. He was so close.

When I met Ron he was driving a Pontiac car, and had been doing so for quite some time. I forget the year but that is not important. He had, at one time a funny odor in the car so he decided to use some oil of wintergreen. Now a few drops would have been just fine, but I think he used far too many drops.

We were on our way to Herman's house for a practice. It was in the winter and I was in the back seat. The heater was on and the smell in the back, was pure wintergreen, and the tears were flowing down my cheeks. I mentioned that it was just a little strong, and he replied, "I can hardly smell it at all now, you should have been with me when it was real strong." I guess I met him at the right time.

A few years ago we persuaded Ron to come out golfing with us. Now we are not the best golfers in the world, but we do have fun. The first time we went Ron just walked along with us, but after that, we convinced him to play along. It was during this time that we were blessed with Herman's expertise on the course.

We were playing an a great little course, called the Fish Pond Golf club. (now closed). I will never forget that day. It was very hot, but pleasant. Herman had hit a great drive off of a par five hole. Now I should tell you just a little about Herman's approach to golf. Herman did not address the ball in a normal fashion. Instead he would walk up to the ball and hit it all in the same motion. If you were near him you had to be very careful, as he would hit the ball before you could find cover. On this occasion, on the par five he did just that on his second shot. It went into the woods and hit a tree. I was on the fairway waiting when he hit the ball for his third shot. The sound that followed was like that of a pinball machine, as his ball hit at least five trees before it came to rest. Still in the rough. I was on my knees laughing, as were the other guys.

That was just one of many days we spent together, that will never be forgotten. We have not golfed for awhile but I think we are due for some more real soon. Ron took to golf quite well and seemed to be a natural even if he did hit left handed.

While we are on the golf kick lets talk about Nick. We invited him along on one of our trips and he just walked along with us. We were in Pictou County, at a great little course. I think we had Ron, Doug, Herman and myself. And Nick as a walk along. After about five holes of terrible golf by all of us, we all had a great tee shot off of the sixth hole. After the last guy hit his ball, Nick spoke up. " I am glad you guys finally hit a good ball off of the tee. I was getting embarrassed just walking with you." He paid for that remark many times over.

Later Nick got some clubs and joined us for a game or two. I put this in Ron's chapter because he seems to be the one who laughs about it the most.

Figure 4 Ron at Possum Lodge.

Chapter Seven: Moments to remember.

Since I began to play the fiddle, there have been many fond memories. Some of these I will relate to you as we go along.

I grew up in the Musquodoboit Valley and attended school there. My first four years were in a two room school, called, Henry School. The school is gone now but I have a few memories, and a clear picture in my mind of the actual school. It was during this time that I went to, and competed in a regional music festival. I don't have many memories of the festival other than the fact I was very nervous. I do remember riding about twelve miles to the festival in the back of a truck on dirt roads. I had on my Sunday suit which was dark blue when I left, and very brown with dust, when I arrived.

When I was going into grade five, my family moved a couple of miles down the road, and I had to change schools. I was to be a student of a, one room school, in Hutchinson Section. At that time the school areas were called Sections. In a radius of twenty miles there would be at least eight or ten sections, in the valley.

I started high school in grade seven and attended Musquodoboit Rural High School, in Middle Musquodoboit. That first day was very scarey for me. I left a school, that had about twenty children, to go to a new one, with three hundred and twenty five. It was the most people I had ever seen in one place in my life. I found most of the teachers very strict and I came home crying more than once in those first few days. I did not say anything at home as I thought it was something I would have to handle on my own. I did, and I later learned to respect the teachers I had. I think a small amount of fear is good for us at times.

Before too long I began to feel at home there and had many happy days before I left. Those days were some of the best days of my life. I studied music there, or should I say I attended music class. At one point I joined the glee club and believe it or not I became quite a singer. It was at this school that I would meet Henry Moore, a very good fiddler. I remember him bringing his fiddle to school and playing during lunch break and any other time that was available. It was many years after I left school that our paths crossed again. Henry is one of the best fiddlers in our area and plays for a lot of events.

51

Many years later, after we started playing for various functions, I was delighted when we were asked to play at an anniversary there and later a school reunion dance. The reunion had to be the biggest highlight for me as I was going back to my old school. We spent the day meeting with old school mates and, reminiscing. It had been over fifty years since I left.

During the day there were many old memories that came to mind. Seeing so many people that I had not seen for many years. A trip to Mr. Blackburn's shop was a real treat, talking about the happy hours I spent there building and laughing. It was the best room in the school for me and that day was no exception. Another event that came to mind was one of our dances in the gym when we were members of Allied Youth. I was trying to dance with a lady I had taken a fancy to. The tune was the Tennessee waltz. I know I was not doing well, but she hurt me deeply when she said," you are too stupid to learn how to dance." It was many years later that I learned to dance, and proved her wrong.

When our reunion dance started that evening, fifty years later, the lady who called me stupid was there. We made it a point to play the Tennessee waltz. I had thought of going down and asking her for the dance, but my better judgement prevailed. Sometimes when people put you down it gives you an incentive to achieve greater things. For that I guess I should thank her.

The evening was one of our best performances, and for me a chance to play some good old time music for my old school buddies. Very shortly after we played there, the school was torn down to make way for another in its place. To the best of my knowledge we were the last people to play for an old time dance at that location.

Another proud moment for me was playing for my father. When I first started taking lessons, I decided to keep this from my father and then play a tune for him to surprise him. I decided I would play, silent night, as Christmas was drawing near. I practised for days and finally I got my chance. I took the fiddle to his home and played the tune as a gift for him. It brought tears to his eyes. I am not sure if I was that good or, that bad.

Less than a year later he passed away. So many times I procrastinate, but this time I did something before it was too late.

My Mother-in-law, Ena MacKay Dean was one of our biggest fans. She loved our music and travelled many miles to hear us play and have a dance or two. When we made our fist recording she sold more than the rest of us put together. She would call us every few days and say, " bring more tapes the next time you come up" She would always insist on paying for them up front. I am sure she gave a lot away just to get our music out there. She was very proud of her daughter and the rest of the band.

My Father-in-law, George A Dean, was no less a fan, he loved the old traditional tunes and he was a great dancer. He would listen to us, and say it reminded him of his uncle Win. He had a favourite tune, Four Strings and I, that he loved to hear. It is no doubt the two of them encouraged us to continue

Being able to take part in any event for charity has always been my main objective. There is always a sense of accomplishment when you can help others and enjoy the trip. We have done this countless times and it is still the best way to get a, Rush.

One of my favourite places to play is, the Braeside home for special care in Middle Musquodoboit. Perhaps because it is close to my old homestead, but it always seems to be filled with warmth and loving care. We have made it our objective to spend as much time as we can to help support them with our music. I can't say enough for the entire staff of this facility. When we play there it is very rewarding to see the residents respond to our music. It is even more important to see the way the staff treats the residents every day. If and when I reach that point in time that I can not be taken care of at home, I would be delighted to go to Braeside.

We recently took part in a concert in Shubenacadie, at the united church. It is a beautiful facility and the acoustic's are great. What a joy to see people come from such a distance to help support a cause. The church was almost full, and they were well entertained. Many fiddlers took turns, all with the help of great accompaniment. I was the lucky one to play first, and then relax to the sweet music of the others.

It is events like this that make one realize how many talented people there are in our area. Just think of the money we pay to hear others who are not a bit better. I am not just talking about fiddle music.

For every style of music, there are many who have great talent, and yet they seem to be overlooked. I have always been one to cheer for local talent. How can we ever develop our talent if we don't support it.

Because our hobby is music we see many people who play just for their own enjoyment, however with a little encouragement they play in front of an audience, and learn to enjoy that as well. It is very rewarding to help people learn, and show their talent. No matter what the occasion, when you plan an event you should look closest to home for your entertainment.

Thelma Marie's Waltz

By Robert
Taylor

The music at the side is a waltz I wrote for my sister, Thelma Marie. She died of cancer at the age of 54. I think about her often, as we were very close.

She was the best dancer in our family, and loved the down east music. I am sorry I never got a chance to play for her, but there are times when I feel she is listening.

I have many fond memories of the laughter we shared when we were young. I will always remember her sense of humour.

Thelma was never blessed with good eyesight and in later years she became almost totally blind. This did not slow her down, nor did she complain. It seemed her hearing senses got much better to help compensate for her loss of sight. She could pick up the slightest noise, and the sound of a voice was very clear to her.

I remember one occasion when she came home from Ontario for a visit. She brought her son and two daughters with her, but on one Saturday evening she asked me to escort her to the community hall for the weekly old time dance. (Music supplied by Mel McPhee and his band). I was delighted to do so and off we went. On the way she made one request. You see there was a gentleman that always went to the dances who was not a very good dancer. She was not sure if she could see him in the dark hall so she asked me to point him out if I saw him. That way she would have time to avoid him. I kept a look out for him for a short time but soon I had other people to look for. I glanced out on the floor and there she was dancing with the guy she wanted to avoid. When the music stopped I went to her and told her, that was the guy you did not want to dance with. She replied, " you jerk you were supposed to look out for me" We had many laughs about that incident later in life.

My whole family have been very close even though we do not see each other very often. My oldest brother, Stewart is a story teller just like our father. He has provided me with many laughs over the years.

On one occasion quite a few years ago he was hitchhiking from Halifax to his home in Bridgewater. He was in the Navy at the time, and did not have a car. He would stay in Halifax and work for the week and then go home on the weekends. While he was hitchhiking a guy came along in a, Prefect car, (Small English vehicle). The drive was so fast Stewart was scared out of his wits. He did make it however and lived to make another trip. The next week he was again hitching a ride when he saw the same car approaching. He ran and hid in the bushes until the guy had passed by.

The broken step.

Another story he told, had taken place in the same Henry School that I attended in later years. Stewart so I am told, by his old classmates was very smart, but studying was not one of his strong points. He did however do very well in school, in spite of his urge to raise hell.

I have heard this story from two sources and both versions seem to be almost the same. On some occasions when the boys would get tired of their sandwiches they had brought from home, they would take them down to the furnace in the basement, at lunch time and toast them over the hot coals. Now this was a splendid way to add a little zest to their lunch. There was, however one major flaw in this practice. The teacher would smell the smoke as they would have to open the door to the furnace. On this one occasion they were ready for her. They knew she would come down and put a stop to their warm lunch so they took steps to discourage her from doing so anytime soon. There was a dirt floor in the basement and for some reason there was always a puddle of water just at the foot of the stairs. It was quite dark there so they devised a plan. They would remove one of the steps quite near to the bottom. It is not quite clear which one of these boys performed this task. The teacher did smell the smoke and even if it was lunch time she called for the boys to return to the class. They did not answer. She called again saying, "If you boys do not come up here I will go down after you" They remained quiet and soon she was on her way down the stairs. As she was not used to the dark she did not see the missing step. She plunged face first into the water hole. Now I did not get all the details from this point on only to hear that she was muddy but not hurt. One of these boys went on to Medical school and has now retired from medicine. He did tell me they actually felt sorry for the poor teacher.

Now I realize that this story like a lot of others does not have a noticeable connection to music. The point is however that there is a connection. I was at a church hall playing music when this story was related to me. In fact every thing in this book has a tie to music. When I reflect on my life I am amazed at the number of things that have been connected to music , even long before I started to play.

There are many stories I have heard from my siblings, all of which are true, with a little colour added. This is another one that involved my two oldest brothers. It all started on a train ride we took to visit some of our relatives in Ontario. Our first ride was when I was the child of the trio, at 69 years. My brother Keith was 79 and Stewart was 82. It was on this occasion the we solved many world problems. During one of our discussions the subject of bulling came up. Stewart said, "we did not have bullies when we were young." Keith replied, "then what would you have called it when you made Donald Archibald eat Sheep Manure"? Stewart replied that perhaps they did have bullies after all.

The world is rapidly changing but perhaps the old saying is correct. The more things change the more they are the same. Schooling was certainly tough when we were young, but lessons learned the tough way seem to stick a lot longer. In spite of the tricks they played on others, I am sure they were on the receiving end on many occasions. I am very proud of my siblings and I hope they feel the same way about me. Yes we are from the old school, and tough times made us strong.

Vivian and I have tried to give our children a lot of things we did not have when we were growing up. Not because we were ever in need, but because times were changing and we wanted to provide them with a slightly better quality of life. I honestly believe we succeeded, even if we still wish we could have given them more.

Our three sons are grown now and have their own responsibilities. Each generation lives in a newer world with more and more pressure to succeed. That is why it is so important to take time in our busy lives to appreciate the special moments, and to pass them on to others. I have had many special moments and many special friends. I think of them quite often as a way to brighten my days.

I thank my family for a lot of very special moments and have always had one wish. I want my family to love and respect their parents as I have mine. If we all strive to do that and succeed, the world will be a better place.

If you were to ask each member of our band what music has done for them I am sure they would all agree. Special moments, and special friends

When we travel from place to place we meet a lot of great people. Sometimes we will run across a person who is a bit of a pain. I don't want to go into any great detail because this book is meant to be positive. I say this because they are real and we have to contend with them. The picture on the next page sums it up quite well.

Figure 2 As we travel through life we meet a lot of these, but they too help build character.

This was a test. I hope you passed.

Chapter Eight.

Malcolm Douglas Nicholson

Born May 15th 1937 in Eldon P.E.I.

Get the facts then you can distort them as much as you like
Mark twain.

I was born in Prince Edward Island just outside the village of Eldon. In a farm house along the present Trans Canada Highway. Besides our parents there were five girls and three boys in our family. We lived on a farm with a view of Nova Scotia across the Northumberland Strait. At night you could see car lights, and I wondered who lived over there. In a few years I found out.

When I was about eight years old an older brother bought a guitar at Eaton's. It was black with a picture of   the lone Ranger and Tonto on the top. He soon became tired of trying to play. I guess it was too hard on his fingers.

One day a local musician stopped by. He tuned the guitar and sang some songs. The only one I can remember was the "Blue Tailed Fly" From then on I was hooked. Things didn't go well, for, by now the guitar was out of tune. Luckily a new brother-in-law arrived on the scene. He was very musical and tuned it up every time he visited.

After learning some chords, a cousin taught me when to change from one chord to another. The first song I was able to play was an old Hymn, "At the Cross, At the Cross, Where I first Saw The Light"

My cousin's father was the Light House Keeper at Pt. Prim P.E I.

Figure 1 Nick with Big Bertha.

59

Graham Townsend wrote the well known tune ," The Light House Keeper, for him " I have lost touch with my cousin and have not found out how he got to know Mr. Townsend. My cousin and his father were both named , Angus Murchison and lived in Pt. Prim.

In 1957 I joined the RCAF and after Trades Training I was stationed in Trenton Ontario. A short time later I joined a band called, "The Sunset Ramblers" We played for square dances in the local area. A highlight for our band was the nine weeks we had, a half hour radio show on a small station in Colborne Ontario.

While at Trenton I heard Ward Allen play for a, dairy association dance in the Bellville Arena. Over the years I have heard many great fiddlers, but Ward was the greatest in my Book.

After postings in Summerside P.E.I. Lahr Germany, and Greenwood N.S. our family, Wife Ellen, Daughters Sheila, and Mary and I moved to Enfield N.S. in July 1984. Later on I started playing with the Metro Fiddlers, and lately with the Down Home Fiddlers. It was during these years that I met up with members of the Last Chance Band, finally joining them in the summer of 1995.

In the thirteen years plus since playing with , Last chance, there are many memories and highlights that come to mind. I can sum it up by saying that when the practice night comes around I look forward to seeing the gang and playing our music. As much as, I did the very first time.

Figure 2 The Sunset Ramblers.

Meeting Nick, and having the privilege of playing with him has been a great experience for me. He has been everything anyone could ask for as a band member. He is a great Guitar, and Stand Up Bas player. He is steady. By this I mean his playing is always constant. No big highs or lows like a lot of others. He plays well and has a great beat.. He is always there for the band. It takes severe weather or very urgent circumstances to keep him away. In all the years we have played and the many places we have traveled I have yet to hear him say, "I don't want to go" He is a Team player and you have heard me say before how important that is.

Shortly after we first met Nick, his wife Ellen suffered a setback after a Heart operation. For a long period of time she was in Hospitals and, a Home for Special care. She passed away without ever returning to their home in Enfield. This was a very difficult time for our friend Nick, but he never seemed to let it show. We all tried to be there for him and help keep his spirits up. We did not talk about the stress he must have been under, but I hope he knew just how much we felt for him. We only knew Ellen for a short time, but we soon realized she could keep one step ahead of Nick. They seemed to have fun together.

Figure 3 My first Car.

The Cherry Pie.   I remember the supper our group was invited to as a thank you. We had played for a reception at the Via Rail Station in Halifax. For Ralph and Grace Scott. They had prepared a delicious meal at their house a few days after the reception. Nick and Ellen were there along with the rest of our group. We had a special fried chicken and Cherry pie for desert. The pie was the best I ever had. We questioned her on the recipe, but she just said it was one of her own. Nick was beside himself with this pie as well. As we were leaving, he offered his keys to Ellen and said, "You can go home now I am staying right here". I guess he had that pie on his mind. We still talk about that meal.

The New Shoes   Nick is normally very quiet, but as you get to know him, you see another side. He has a very dry sense of humor and uses it to keep us laughing on many occasions. There have been many stories he has told that seem funny only when he tells them. One of these is a story we shall call, the shinny shoes. When Nick was quite young his Mother bought him a pair of shinny black shoes. Now Nick was very proud of these shoes and got permission from his Mother to wear them over to the neighbors house to show them off. When he arrived he went right in to see the lady of the house. She told them how nice they looked, and that he should go out to the barn and show them to the hired hand, who was milking the Cows. Nick decided to do this as he knew the young man quite well. He chose his steps very carefully and proceeded towards the barn. As he arrived at the barn door, he looked in and saw the man milking one of the cows. He hollered, "what do you think of my new shoes?" The man looked around and without a word, took aim and squirted milk all over Nick's new shoes. You could say this sort of took the shine off of the new footwear.

          It is not a well known fact but Nick is a good singer. On many occasions we have tried in vain to get him to sing. It is very rare that he will break out in song. Once or twice when we would be resting at Possum Lodge, he would come out with a line or two. One that comes to mind, is a couple of lines he gave us while strumming the Guitar." I wanted to be a Cowboy, but I was always afraid of Cows."

The Roast Beef

Several years ago we were asked to play for my cousin, Harold and Mildred Whidden.'s wedding anniversary in New Glasgow. As we were on a low budget, and our Cottage was near by at Melmerby Beach we decided to stay there. The following day I roasted a big piece of beef. Ellen and Nick were there as well along with most of our group. When the meal was served and everyone was commenting on the tender beef, Nick asked, " What did you say this was? Did you call it meat?" I assured him it was in fact meat. He turned to Ellen and said. " Ellen we have got to try this some time, I did not know there was such a

Figure 4 Point Prim Light P.E.I.

thing. We have laughed at this one a few times as well, knowing full well that Nick was never left out when it came to good food.

Shortly after Nick joined our band, he asked me if I knew where he could get a, stand up Bas. As it turned out I did know where there was one for sale. It was in Ontario. My Nephew Douglas Miller's Mother-in-law had one. My Sister Frances and her Husband were coming home that summer, and agreed to bring it along with them. (They had a big Car.)

I was to meet them when they arrived at my brother's house and pick it up. After a short visit with my Brother, I made the comment that I should load Big Bertha In my van. My Sister Frances started to laugh at this remark. You see the original owner's name was Bertha. From that day on Nick's Bass has been known as, **Big Bertha.**

On the previous page a picture of Point Prim Light. Graham Townsend wrote a tune called, "The Lighthouse keeper" and this is the lighthouse it was named for. Angus Murchison was the keeper of this light for many years. He was related to Nick.

Another funny story Nick related to us at Possum Lodge. When he was quite young back home on the farm, his father would have to make trips to town from time to time for supplies. Nick and other members of the family would quite often ask if they could go along. He would often reply by saying, " yes someday". This went on for quite some time until Nick heard his brother ask if he could go. Father said, " Ok we will go someday" Nick jumped at the chance and asked the same question. He got the same reply. "Yes we will go someday" Nick was a bit upset and replied to his father. "But that's the same day my brother is going. I wanted to go a different day."

Chapter Nine: Special People In My Life.

When we play in Upper Musquodoboit, we often have, the Rev Gary Burrill Join us. He is very capable of playing several instruments and enjoys them all. His whole family are great Musicians. His youngest Daughter is an exceptional fiddle player and also joins us from time to time.

Gary has been the Minister in the area for several years. I am not sure, but I think his stay may have outlasted all others in the recent past. I have known Gary for several years and have the highest regard for him and his outlook on life. He Has what I will refer to as, as a very modern approach to his messages. He is very liberal, (not necessarily in the political sense), and serves the community with an energetic force. Since the beginning of this book, Gary has become a Provincial MLA for the New Democratic Party. My congratulations go out to this fine gentleman. He will be a fine politician.

It seems that I have seen him at funerals more often than any other place. He has a special way of talking to the families who have lost their loved ones. I always marvel at his ability to draw your attention towards the deceased, in such a warm and thoughtful manner. I spoke to him very recently about this subject and complemented him on the sensitive manner he has. We also spoke of the stress, he must go through, when he has so many funerals in a short span. He said it was true, and that is why he loves to join us when we play. Music is a wonderful way to relax. I should also point out that Gary and part of his family play for a dance in the same hall we do. They play on the third Saturday of the Month.

While I no longer live in the area, I do get to see Gary quite often. He has become a very good friend of everyone in our band and we welcome his presence any time.

This brings me to my Dad again, a very strong influence on my life. He was a Baptist, but favoured the United Church. Now some would say he was not a religious man, because he did not attend Church. They did not know my Father like I did. I remember when I was going to school, and Sunday would come around, I would be off to Sunday School first and then Church. He made me go, or shall I say he encouraged me to go, or else. When my Stepmother and the rest of the family left for Church, he would start to prepare Dinner. This was a ritual with him on Sundays. There is one other thing he did, that not many people knew about. He would turn on the radio and listen to a Church service. I know this because on more than one occasion I ran home and surprised him. He would just smile and turn the radio down.

When there was work to be done at the Church he was always willing to do more than his share. He gave money each week, even when times were very hard. Was he a religious man? Much more so than a lot of people who attended Church every Sunday. I tell you this story because it ties in with Gary Burrill.

I remember being at home when one of our previous Ministers came to visit for the first and last time.(He will remain nameless). He knocked on the door and Dad invited   him in. Shortly after he came in, Dad reached for his cigarettes and offered one to the new Minister. Oh my he said, "a good Minister would never smoke." Well knowing my Dad , I decided to get to another room where it was safe, but stay close enough for the fireworks. Because they were going to fly any moment. Well! said my Dad, " I have known Minister's much better than you who smoked two packs a day." So after a few awkward moments the new Minister excused himself, and to the best of my knowledge he must have taken our name off his list, for he never called again.

My Father passed away before, Rev. Gary Burrill arrived on the scene, however he always liked to meet the new Minister, soon after he arrived. I have often tried to picture the scene, If Gary were to arrive when my father was still alive. My father would have had a Tiger by the tail and they would both be laughing. He was a very kind and gentle

Man, but he loved to tease, especially if he liked you. Gary my good friend, he would have loved you.

Dad was a great story teller as well. He could take a true story and make it spellbinding. He also had a tremendous ability to help others along with a story if he knew they were stretching the truth. When I was a young boy at home I loved the fireside stories told by my parents and friends. One night when one of the friends was in for a visit, he started telling a story about a logging camp that he worked at. He told us that the cook had to carry in, a one hundred pound bag of flour, every day, and two, one hundred pound bags of sugar a week, just to make enough Pancakes for breakfast. Without hesitation , Dad said," Oh I remember that camp. The stove was so big he fried the Pancakes on top of the stove without a frying Pan. He used to tie Pork Rinds to his feet and skate on the stove to grease it up. This was Dads Way of saying, "It's a good story but not a word is true"

On another occasion, when our Aunt Fanny was visiting, he added to one of her stories, But first I have to tell you about Aunt Fanny. She was my Step-Mothers aunt who came to stay with us in the summer for at least two months. She was a joy to have around and she filled our days with laughter. She was a little old lady with bowed legs like a Chimpanzee. Her hearing was bad, and she could break wind at will. Now for a young boy that was exciting.

Back to my story. We were at the dinner table and she was telling dad about some old gent from the community who loved his tea, hot. She said "He had to have his tea boiling when it was put in his cup, and he never took milk" Just then Father said, "yes I know and he put red hot irons in it as well to keep it hot." Aunt fanny exclaimed, "Well I did not know that, for heavens sake, I did not know that"

There was another story about our dear Aunt Fanny, I should mention. She was a very dear lady and had a special love for my brother Dennis. When he was about eight years old, she had come to visit for one of her summer stops. There was a canteen just up the road from our house and she would walk up there quite often. Now Dennis knew her habits, and watched for her return. He knew she would have a treat for him. He waited until he saw her walking down the road, and then set out to meet her. When he got close to her he ran and jumped up in her arms, and toppled her right over into the ditch. She did have candy for him and it flew all over the ground. She was not hurt in any way, and the candy was saved, but Dennis still feels sorry for that day. We often laugh about it now and think of poor Aunt Fanny. She was a treasure, and we will remember her all the days of our lives. You may see other stories of her later on.

You will read more about my Dad later on too, as he was a very important part of my growing up. When I was six years's old my Mother passed away. My Dad was left with seven children to provide for in very tough times. I as the youngest and of course needed the most attention. Dad worked hard at keeping the family together, and my older brother's and sister's helped out as best they could. I think it made us all closer together to this day.

I remember many things about my Mother. And to this day I get flash backs to those hard times, but good times. I remember part of a poem she had and it has come to my mind many times in my life. "**One must stand in the deepest darkness to see the brightest light, and out of our very own darkness comes the brightest light.**" There was more to it but that is the part that comes back to me quite often.

Several years later my Dad remarried and I was given the best Step-Mother one could ever ask for. They had one son, Dennis. I guess the term they use is half brother when they explain the relationship between Dennis and the rest of my brothers and sisters. To me he will always be our brother.

One of the people in my childhood who impressed me the most was, My Great Aunt Martha. She lived in Sunny Brae, Pictou County. She was the kindest person I ever met. I always looked forward to the trips to her house. She was my Mothers aunt, my Grandmothers sister, and she could bake the best biscuits and cookies I ever ate. She would give me these with a big glass of buttermilk. I will never forget those days.

I used to go in the summer for a few weeks with two of my sisters Frances and Thelma. Aunt Martha was married, but she did not have any children of her own. She did however raise four young girls who were her sisters children. Her sister passed away when the girls were all very young. These four girls and my two sisters were all about the same age but older than I was. Here I was with six ladies plus my aunt Martha looking after me. No wonder I loved Sunny Brae so much. Then there was Uncle Jim. He worked all day, and smiled all evening. He would set in his chair in the kitchen, smoke his pipe and Smile.

Many years later I wrote a Song called, The Hills Of Sunny Brae. It was my small way of saying thank you to my aunt and cousins who made me feel at home. and also describing the beautiful Village. I still go there every few years, just to get the rush, The old house

is gone now, and nothing looks the same, but I have the memories. I can stand where the old house used to be and almost smell the Biscuits.

Figure 1   Aunt Martha's House. Note the road in front.

I have been told that this old house once provided over night lodging for British Royalty in the 1800 hundred's. As far as I am concerned the Royalty was there as long as Aunt Martha was there. I know we can't go back, but if we could, you would see me at the door. At some point in everyone's life there should be an Aunt Martha.

In my life I have had so many good friends and relatives, and they come to mind, quite often. I will not be able to tell you about all of them but perhaps I could mention one couple that had a great influence on my life. That would be my Grandparents, Corey Taylor and Susan MacLeod Taylor

They lived in Wittenburg Nova Scotia. In the summer I would visit for a couple of weeks, along with my brothers and sisters. Wittenburg at that time was a small village with several small children. There was so much to do there, and everyone seemed so carefree. I had many cousins to play with and I was under the watchful eye of my Grandmother .She was a warm hearted lady, who made sure we got lots to eat and lots of rest.

My grandfather was a quiet man who was busy all day just keeping the grounds looking nice. After supper he would take me out to the front veranda and, here he would light his pipe and tell me stories. I would be all ears as he was so interesting. He spoke very softly so I had to set very close so I would n't miss a word.

One of the stories he told was of his walk from Labrador to Quebec City. A total of twenty one days. I have a copy of his diary that I cherish. It was not until later years that I realized just how difficult this must have been.

On one occasion I ventured out with some of my cousins to a lumber mill down the road. It was exciting for a young boy to watch the old steam mill saw through the logs and listen to the sounds of the old engine. While we were there, the cook from the camp invited us in for a piece of pie. She filled us up with pie and cookies until we could just barely walk. When I got back to my grandparents, it was almost time for supper. My appetite was not at its best for the meal and grandmother scolded me and told me I could not run around all day and not eat. I did not say a word but grandad winked and I think he knew why I could not eat much that night.

One night after supper I learned a very lasting lesson from my grandmother. It was thundering, and the lightning was very bright. I was scared but I did not want them to know. She saw my tears and put her arm around me and took me to the door. The backdoor was in the kitchen and it had a small porch with a roof over it. The rain was pouring down off of the porch. She said to me. "Do you see all that rain?" I told her I did and she said. " Don't ever be afraid of the thunder storms when it is raining." I felt better right away and to this day I think of this every time it thunders.

It is amazing how one small explanation can have such a lasting effect on a person. My grandmother was a kind, and sweet little lady, and she saved me from fear that evening. On a later visit to her house she told me about my fathers first day of school. She had walked him to school, which was about a quarter of a mile. She waited until he went inside the schoolhouse door and then she went back home. When she arrived back home, my father was setting beside the kitchen stove. She walked him to school again, but this time he stayed. I never heard what she said or did to him, but she had the power for sure. My fondest memories of my grandparents home was the smell of Roses. To this day when I smell the old fashioned roses my mind goes back to Grandma's house.
There are so many special people in my life I would have to write several books just to do them justice, but there is one gentleman that I met during my early years in the Postal Service . Vernon G Blois, Waverley Nova Scotia. He was a very remarkable man, who unfortunately passed away at an early age. He became one of my very special friends for many reasons. Vernon was a very funny individual. He could make you laugh when laughter was the furthest thing from your mind. I worked with him at the old Dartmouth Post Office in the late 60's and had the good fortune of being his supervisor on shift work. He had three very prominent characteristics. He was very funny, he was Liberal, and he was a Montreal Canadian fan. Of this you could be sure. When things started to get dull, all one had to do was mention a Conservative, and he was off. I learned the art of enjoying mundane tasks from this man. He   had the gift of lifting people from a low, and making them laugh.

Vernon had a mouth organ, but to say he could play it would be a stretch. Once in a while he would get it out and hit a few sour notes. He would do this until someone would plead with him to stop. I played a lot of Golf with him and Curled for a few years with him . During these events he would always have his mouth organ. It was one of the curling events that we were returning from the rink by taxi. There were four of us with Vern in the middle of the back seat. He started to play, and the taxi driver turned around in his seat and looked with the saddest look I ever saw. Knowing the situation I decided to help matters along. I told the driver he should have heard him before he started taking lessons. We all had a great laugh especially the driver.

In just a few years he died of cancer. He had many friends who were shocked to see him go so soon. This was before I started to play the fiddle, but I think of him each time I hit a bad note. He was a great friend, and he memory will always be with me.

More on Aunt Fanny. I warned you she might appear again in this book. This lady will live in my mind forever.

Many years ago when I was working for the Bank of Nova Scotia in Truro, Nova Scotia I had an opportunity to pick her up at her friend's house and take her to my parents home in Upper Musquodoboit. Now at this time, I was just barely getting by and did not have money for a lot of extra's. I was driving a 1950 Austin car, which I doubt was a reliable car when it was new. We set out for the country and prayed for the best. It was approximately thirty five miles. At that time a large portion of the road was unpaved and the dust came in one end of the car and out the other.

She decided she would set in the back seat and enjoy the ride. After we had been on the road for several minutes, I looked in the rearview mirror and could not see her. At first I was afraid she had somehow fallen out, until I realized she was lost in the dust. We had to travel several more miles before we reached our destination, and I was worried she would choke to death in all that dust. She was not disturbed in the least and when we arrived, she simply shook the dust from her clothing and proceeded towards my parent's house. She had the look of Queen who had just ridden in the Royal Carriage. She would later tell my Father it was a very enjoyable ride.

On another occasion I picked her up at the same location. This time I was driving a different car. I had traded my Austin for a 1950 Plymouth. I thought I was coming up in the world. Not so, that car will remain in my mind as the worst car I ever owned. It did however get me from point A to point B that evening in fine style. I followed the same route as before but with a little less dust. You see this car had bigger holes for the dust to escape. On this journey we travelled up over the Stewart Hill Road. As I was rounding one of the many turns, I saw two racoons in the wheel tracks ahead. Now in those days, racoons had a $2.00 bounty on them. This was a lot of money for a young banker so I tried to hit them. I managed to hit one but the other got away.

I stopped the car and picked up my prey, then continued on my way. While I was speeding and swaying back and forth to hit the racoon, Aunt Fanny did not seem to be too concerned. When we arrived at our destination later that evening, she very quickly told my father about the event. She said "Clifford, Clifford, that son of yours is the best driver I ever knew. When we were coming over Stewart Hill, there were two racoons on the road. He did all he could to avoid hitting them but he did hit one. He managed to keep the car on the road, and oh my he is a good driver".

My father just smiled at her and gave me a wink. He knew what my intentions were. That was many years ago and today I would go to any lengths to avoid hitting even a caterpillar.

It has also been many years since our dear Aunt Fanny left us, but I will always remember her and her little putt, putt, putt as she would climb the stairs to her room at the end of each day. She was a kind lady and we loved her. It always seemed to me she was a young lady in an old lady's body, but at that time I was a young boy who thought he was a man.

And in the end, it's not the years in your life that count. It's the life in your years.   *Abraham Lincoln.*

Another special person in my life was my sister Mildred. She lived in Halifax in a small apartment. She lived a simple life and would never hurt a soul. Give her a dollar and you can bet she would save half of it. If she were running our country there would not be a deficit. A very sweet lady who knew all of her relatives, and could tell you their birthdays at random. We could all learn from her.

Figure 2 Mildred and Malcolm Taylor (twins). My Sister and Brother about 1940. They are both gone now.

Chapter Ten Doug Morash

Music is moonlight in the gloomy night of life.   Jean Paul Richter.

Music was always in our home around a player piano. Neighbors played fiddle and I enjoyed the music but never thought I would play. At an early age I started piano lessons but like most young boys was not interested in spending a lot of time practicing.

Later in life I did go back to piano and took a year or more lessons, then switched to organ and then gave up. It wasn't until many years later I was visiting a friend's cottage and before going to bed that night he played a few tunes on the fiddle and from that time I was hooked. Although realizing I would never be a fiddler of great merit I have enjoyed every minute of the trip.

Sunday night was music time at our home around the piano with neighbors and sing songs. During my early youth I participated in Natal Day parades, Community Fairs and in teenage years at dances in the local hall. Plays put on by Church Youth Groups, Cubs and Scouts.

In Adult year's a lot of time was spent working and Square Dancing as well as running Youth Groups at the school and later in the community. While working I proceeded to study and obtain my accounting designation so there was not too much free time for many social activities.

I recall a highlight of my early teens was the bicycle races held annually at our local community hall and the race course was from Porto Bello back to the hall. I bought my first bike (used) for the great sum of $10.00 and was ready for the race. Don't remember if I was in the first 20 finishers or not but I got a prize, being a flashlight and that made the day. In those days the RCMP were our course marshals.

Highlights of being part of the Last Chance Band: Just having the opportunity   to be a member of a group of players like   those in the band was the highlight of my exposure. I do not know where you will find a

 group of people of varied backgrounds that are so understanding, compatible and willing to help one another. We have enjoyed many wonderful outings together even when one forgets the beans and then by talking out loud get's a new "Nick Name" Our trips to Nursing Homes , Anniversaries, Possum Lodge and various Golf Games have also helped in making the bond stronger.

We have been fortunate in having a very loyal group of supporters who love our music and I would venture to say we are one of a very few Old Time Dance Bands in the Metro area. Would you believe this all started from one outing at the Dartmouth Ferry Terminal a number of years ago at which time we had met one another on other occasions but never even considered forming a group.

Our aim has been to provide Good dance music and to raise funds for Charity, our time is free and we have supported Christmas Daddies, Canadian Cancer, and persons in need through funds raised by playing I wish to thank all who have made the Last Chance Band possible

Doug Morash the worker. This is the best way to describe this individual. He was one of the original six members in our band. and probably the one most determined to improve. Always on hand to do his share of the work and that of, several others. Sometimes he tries so hard to help, he gets in his own way.

I remember one night we were packing our gear in Upper Musquodoboit, after a dance. This was one of the occasions when Doug could not make it. Now to understand the situation you will have to know it was always a race to see how quick we could get on the road. We finished and were leaving the Hall just thirteen minutes after we finished the last waltz. Herman declared we set a new record, and also had an explanation for it. In his very own words," Doug was not here to get in our way."

On another occasion Herman said it was much safer to set on the sidelines and watch Doug load the gear himself than risk being hit with a mike stand or get wrapped up in a cord of wire. It would be hard to imagine Doug employed in a fancy china shop. But then again it would be great to have on video.

Yes we tease him a lot and he is one of a kind but he is truly a good worker and a friend .Doug would be the first to admit it is a struggle to learn new tunes without the music in front of him, however he has a tenacious attitude toward learning. We could all improve a great deal more if we adopted just a measure of this. He does not limit his efforts to just, our group.

He has been, and still is, involved in many activities I am sure he gives his all in these other duties as well. I have worked with him on several occasions, and always see the same performance.

This may come as a surprise to you readers to find out that, as hard as he works he can relax in the same fashion. "See figure three."On more than one occasion when we have gone on one of our trips to play Golf or just some R & R at Possum Lodge, He relax's in style. Once again when all the household chores are finished he departs to his bunk, and, in a flash is entertaining the rest of us with the snore, equal to a thousand Camels. We have tried several things to muffle the sound, however he is still the Champ. Please do not get the impression that he is the only one to make the loud noises. On rare occasions one or two of us will try to compete, but he will always be number one..

In our group Nick names abound. Doug is one of the members with several. Boom, Boom is one of them Another is D. H. (Explanations will appear in other parts of the book)

Figure 2 Nick, Isabelle Conrad, and Doug. Following a Church Fiddle Service in Upper Musquodoboit.

77

Figure 3 Doug Morash. Can't keep him still

Case of the missing Beans.

We had planned a golf trip to Parsboro Nova Scotia, and everyone was given a list of things to take along. We had several meals to provide, and this crew can eat their share. As we were over half way there, Doug announced that he had forgotten the baked beans he had promised to take. We decided not to give him a hard time for this. However just after we arrived at the Cottage, his wife Betty called. During the conversation she mentioned her making Beans especially for us. We heard her call Doug a, D- - k Head. This is the only part we heard loud and clear. Well after we got done laughing we all knew he now had a new nickname. We shortened it to, DH.

Later on we would call him Shorts, but that is another story.

Figure 4 Doug, Herman, and Rob, After a hard day of Golf.

Chapter Eleven: The Story of Possum Lodge.

You have, by now, heard of the Lodge called Possum. It was built in 1994 by the Taylor Boys and Friends. In it's short existence it has heard many tales of heroic's and laughter. There are many tale's that have been told, many times over, and a few that will never be told.

The Last Chance band make it a point to go there at least twice a year. All except Vivian as she

Figure 1   Possum Lodge in the
Spring

would feel rather uncomfortable there with six or seven, farting men. She does have her trips with her friends as well, however and I am sure she enjoys herself just as much as we do. She belongs to a water-fit group and they travel a lot together. For us it is a chance to get away for a few days and relax.

I told you about the water boy story, but I don't think I mentioned the fireman we had. When we go there we always have a few household chores for everyone. On one of our first trips Al volunteered to keep the fire burning. This includes nights as well. He said when he got up in the night he would put a stick or two in the stove. That would have been fine except for the fact he was up at least five times. Well I was closest to the source of heat and by five in the morning I felt like I was a fresh biscuit ready to come out of the oven.

Ron Dares was in one of the top bunks and said when awoke in the early morning he was sure he had died and gone to Hell. We decided that morning over breakfast that Al would be signed other duties, post haste. There have been so many funny stories, I could fill another book.

There is one other that I should tell about myself, and my complete lack of knowledge at times. I had gone back to the lodge with a good friend of mine from Ontario. Warren Brown and his wife Irene come home from Ontario every summer for about five months. They have a pretty little trailer site down on the main road in Dean. Warren had mentioned that he would like to have some small poles to make a fence. Since I had more than I would ever use, at the camp I told him we would go cut some. He told me he had bought a new chain saw in Ontario he had never used. We also invited another gentlman, Aubrey Rogers. Now Aubrey is the best man with a chain saw I ever met. He could cut a cord of wood while I was filling my saw with fuel. On this day he Was after a few windfalls for stove wood.

Figure 2 Budd and Doug afraid to go out?

We picked a hot day in July when the bark would peel off the tree without too much effort. Aubrey left us near the camp and went looking for his windfalls. Warren and I decided to start cutting right away, and then we could peel the poles. I started my saw and found a tree just right for our needs. When I tried to cut, the chain jumped off. After several attempts I realized the new chain I had bought was the wrong one for my saw. Not to worry, I thought as Warren had his saw going, and I watched him give it a try. He pressed the saw to the tree as hard as he could but it would not cut.

We discovered that the chain was on backwards. Now I want you to know we were laughing like the fools, we were, but the Black Flies were swarming us and we had to retreat. Just then we heard Aubrey on his way back, You guessed it. He had his truck full of blocks. He stayed and helped us cut a few poles and, off we went to a place, free of Black Flies.

Now Warren and I have been around the woods off and on most of our lives and are capable of doing much better than that, but

80

at least we can get a laugh or two from, time to time. When all is said and done, it is a great day when you can get a good laugh at your own expense. Speak about laughing. Look below.

Figure 3 Al, Nick, Ron, Doug, and Budd. (a fishing trip.)

When Herman was living and able, he loved the Camp. He could spin a yarn or two and kept us all laughing. It has always been my belief that, true stories are the funniest stories and Herman could tell them.

He told us a story about him and his brother Scott, when they hauled Christmas trees to Boston They had decided to do this one season as a means of earning lot's of money, so he said. On their way back from their first trip, they had some mechanical failure on the old number Nine highway between Bangor and Calais Maine. There was a problem with the drive shaft and the truck would not move. One of them had to walk back to the nearest house to get help. They flipped a coin and Herman got to stay in the truck. It was very cold that night and Scott had to walk a long distance before he found anyone.

Herman told us he could start the truck, so he thought he had the best of   the deal. After a few minutes he had to get out and relieve himself. When he went to open the door to get back in he discovered he had locked himself out. It took him about fort five minutes to get the door open. He was just about frozen.

He had just started to get warm when his brother came back. He said to Scott, "Where have you been? I almost froze while you were gone." Scott's reply was, "How could you be cold? You set your ass in the warm truck all the time I was gone ".He said he did not tell his brother about locking himself out.

Story telling has always been one of our hi-lights at the camp. The second hi-light would have to be the food. We all chip in when it comes to the work, however the cooking falls on the shoulders of just one or two. There are obvious reasons for this, one being, survival. These fine gentlemen are al my friends but I would not want to depend on most of them for my every day meals. We stick to the simple meals, but the portions are large.

In the spring of course, we depend on the fish we catch for at least one big feast. We always have a back up just in case. We bring fresh bread and rolls from home and once in a while we have a few pickled eggs.

Salt Cod and Pork Scraps, Corned Beaf and Cabbage, Sauerkraut and Sausage, Venison Stew, Chilli, and many others. Make up our main menus.

Sometimes we even have a small bottle of spirits just in case someone drops in for a visit.

At some point in time the instruments come out and, the wild animals come to dance.

Later on it is nice to hear the silence and look at the brightest stars in the world.

Note. To hear the silence there is a small window of opportunity, between the time the last one speaks and the first one starts to snore.
It is all part of the R & R at the Lodge.

Construction of the Camp started with the falling of the trees, in the spring of 1994. We had the trees sawed right on site with a wood miser mill, owned by Charley Jodrey Dartmouth NS. The lumber was milled

in June and stuck until September. The majority of the camp was complete by late November. It is a log camp but the logs were sawn on three sides six by six by six. It worked out very well and many people have taken advantage of it since it opened.
My three sons, their family, and their friends spend a lot of time there. It is nice that they too appreciate a quiet place to relax.

On more than one occasion we have had people in who had absolutely no respect for others property and they left the main cabin in a terrible mess. It is very unfortunate but that is a risk you take with any camp in the woods. It is not elaborate, but it is special to a lot of people.

Figure 5 Ron, Budd, Nick, and Al. I am taking the picture You know where Doug is.

Figure 4   Breakfast at the Lodge.

My second son Kendall designed and built the gazebo that is pictured on the next page.. It is just below the main camp next to the river. It was prefabricated at his home in Dartmouth. The wood was rescued after Hurricane Yuan, damaged his back yard.

Figure 6 The House that Kendall Built, near the Lodge.

I have often been in this area with my Father-in-law, as this was his land at one time. He was always at his best when he was here. The woods certainly has that stillness and quiet that soothes the soul. It was not until he passed away that I really appreciated just how much he loved his time here. He did get to see the construction of the new camp and was very pleased.

For the Last Chance Band it has been a great retreat. There is another positive side as well. We get to solve so many world problems. On most occasions we play our instruments while we are here, but this is one of the times when we go beyond the music.

It was here that Nick received one of his best pieces of advise from Herman. He said to Nick. "Nick my good friend, let me give you this piece of advise. When you come to a fork in the road, take it."

Chapter Twelve:

Alvin Douglas McVicar Born 1935 in Harrington Quebec
When words fail, music speaks   *Hans Christian Anderson*

Figure 1 Harry McVicar and Al
McVicar 1942.

This is a picture taken about 1942 when I was six years old. Taken
with my brother Harry, who was transferred to Europe in 1942 during
WWII. My brother Harry was wounded three times and died in Holland
where he is buried in Nymagen, Holland

My first interest in music started when I heard Don Messer on
the radio. Something about the fiddle caught my ear and I was hooked
forever. Also the piano played by Waldo Munroe and guitar chording of
Cecil MacEachern convinced me that someday I would play all of these
instruments.

We had a piano at home and many hours were spent sitting on
the piano stool wondering what all those keys were for. With the help an
Aunt, it wasn't long before I was playing chords and whistling tunes at
the same time. Shortly after that a guitar arrived in our home from the

Eaton's Catalogue. It was a "Gene Autry" model ordered in at the great expense of $9.95. The piano was old and battered, the guitar did not have the greatest sound but it was a great pastime, when I wasn't fishing or hunting. Around the time I was 15 I started playing the fiddle with two cousins, one on guitar and the other on piano. We were all self taught. When we played something that did not sound right, we did it over. Before long we were playing every chance we would get. Leslie and Harvey were fine musicians in their own right and I will always be grateful to them for inspiring my love of music.

Later on in life I started playing with the "MacTavish Twins" Ann and Linda. As fiddlers were disappearing rapidly, we were in constant demand for country dances, weddings and any excuse anyone could think of for a party. By now I was influenced by Graham Townsend and Ward Allen, many of their tunes I still enjoy playing.

The most enjoyable stories that I can recall are the are times I was growing up. A young boy, second youngest of a family of ten. Mom and Dad had a country store and Post Office fourteen miles from the nearest town of Calumet Quebec. There was no running water in the house until after I left home to join the R.C.A.F. in 1954

We always had one or two Horses. Dad had a mail route of nine miles each way. He drove the route by car every day in summer and three times a week by horse and cutter in the winter. Although these were hard times they still linger in my mind as loving times shared by a very close and loving family.

Musically, traveling to the fiddle contests in Ontario during July and August is something that everyone

Figure 2 Now Al as a Member of the Last Chance Band.

should experience. Staying in parks whenever you can, consists of socializing via barbecues, jam sessions, etc. In most cases, the contest is secondary. When one contest is over it is hook on and head for the next contest. Pembroke is the "granddaddy" of all contests. What used to be a weekend outing is now a one or two-week stay for many who plan their summer vacation around the Pembroke Contest.

The outdoors has played a big part in my life since I was a small boy. I long for the fishing season in the spring and the hunting season in the fall. To me nothing is nicer than sitting in a canoe, paddling around a lake watching a different species of wildlife. Sometimes I even catch a fish! If I do, that's a bonus for the trip. Autumn is the time of year that I travel to Alberta for a week of hunting with my son and his family. Hunting is a passion with my son as well and it is a chance to have some quality time together.

Being with the Last Chance Band is a very unique experience. Many will think that we show up at dances and parties, play and go home until the next gig comes up. There is more to it than that. The trips to and from wherever we play are always a hoot. The little "barbs' that fly around are always hilarious. These times would not be possible were it not for the comradeship that exists among our group.

There is the two trips a year to "Possum Lodge". These events are certainly all the fun that they are meant to be. In the spring trip there is always a meal of fresh trout, walks in the woods and long story telling sessions. Great fun for all, sprinkled with real events, some dry and some wet, that are conversation pieces held over until the next trip. Now, if we only had someone to keep the lodge warm at night!!

Thursday night is always our jam night, that usually lasts three hours. I always look forward to Thursday. It gives us all a chance to work on our tunes old and new. It all consists of eight people working together as a team. That is what our band is, a team that works hard to ensure that we are as good as we can be and hope that the people and parties that we play for enjoy our music and have fun.

Having said all this, you can see that I lead a very busy life. I enjoy every minute of everything I do. This would not be possible if I did not have the support of my wife Nancy. She is my number one fan in everything I do. I thank her so much for allowing me to do the things that I love. Without her, I could not enjoy the lifestyle that I   have, especially being part of the "Last Chance Band".

Al joined us very shortly after we first got together. He has been a welcome addition. He is our strongest fiddle player and has helped us immensely. He does this by encouragement and never in a negative manner. There are times I am sure he would like to take off on his own so he could play some of the more difficult tunes. But then again, I think he is quite happy where he is.

We all owe a debt of gratitude to Al for his help. He has helped our team and I hope in return we have helped him as well. Since we started to play for dances together, we have all tried to be better dancers. We have succeeded in various degrees and Al has been nicknamed the Dancing Bear. I know who the culprit was that gave him this title but I will not disclose his name, only to say we keep him away from the river when we visit Possum Lodge.

Al has competed in many fiddle contests especially in Ontario. He has judged as well from coast to coast and is highly respected for his judging. He is always game for any type of music event and never refuses unless something very unusual comes up.

He has always been especially mindful of the sick and shut- ins. And visits hospitals quite often. He also loves to walk, and logs many miles a week. He teaches Violin, Piano, and Guitar. We are not quite sure what he does with his free time. He is, like the rest of us, very busy, however I am sure he enjoys it.

He also cooks up a mean meal on the barbecue, and his wife, Nancy can put together great meals as well. We attended one of these dinners not long ago. It was a meal fit for kings. Al had been hunting in Alberta and brought back some fresh Deer meat. Not everyone enjoys this delicacy, but we all did that night. Both Al and Nancy are country folks and grew up when times were rather tough. like the rest of us we appreciate our lives just a little more, because of our leaner years. When we speak of special people, Al will always be on the list.

As I write now, Al is recovering from Heart surgery, and doing very well. He had to postpone all playing for a period of time and we certainly missed him.

Figure 3 Al doing what he does so well, at Possum Lodge.

Figure 4 This is the Old Country Kitchen where my grandparents lived. It was also used on our last recording. I knew Al would like this in his profile.

Chapter Thirteen: Budd Gavel Born in Antigonish June 28th 1940

Get someone else to blow your horn and the sound will travel twice as far. Author unknown.

Figure 1 Budd in his early years.

Started to learn Piano Accordion about 1958 or so with the help of friend and fellow printer, "Skip" (Laurens) LeDrew who loved to play music and played many different instruments. We played at local clubs in Antigonish (Legion, Golf club, Boat Club), also kitchen parties and benefit dances in rural schoolhouses etc. My younger brother Ed also played guitar with us. Began working night shift in the composing room at Halifax Herald in 1969 and retired in 1995. Did not play much music in the years from 1969 to 1999. In '99 decided to take up fiddling as a pastime and enrolled for instruction with Gordon Stobbe for a few years. Later joined a fiddle group which eventually became known as The Down home Fiddlers, where I met up with the members of The Last Chance Band, who also happened to be members of The Down Home Fiddlers group. After a time I was invited to play Accordion occasionally as guest of The Last Chance Band at their monthly dances. This was a great opportunity and experience for me, great music with a great group of musicians eager to help me further my quest to improve musically. Eventually I was invited to join The Last Chance Band. It Has been a wonderfully enlightening experience playing music with these very talented musicians and their great repertoire.

Budd has been a very welcome addition to our group. We, along with our friends are especially glad to have the Accordion music to add to the mix. Budd is also doing very well on the fiddle, but right now his accordion is the strong point. Whenever or wherever we play we always invite others to take part, Budd was one of those people and quickly became part of the fabric of our group. When we first formed our group we did not look at the most talented individuals we could get together. Our main purpose was to get a group who would get along well with each other and jell as a group. We were very fortunate that this happened, and we did learn very quickly.

In Budd's case, he was not only asked because he was good, but perhaps more importantly because of his personality. This is not taking anything from his musical ability, but emphasizing his ability to be a team person. Our modest success has come about because of our teamwork and our ability to make sure all of us form an integral part of the band. It is like making a cake. You don't need a lot of ingredients, but you need the right ingredients. There are a lot of very talented musicians in our area, but not many of them could be blended into our cake.

I have a lot of respect for Budd and his tenacity to do the best he can, and continue to get better every time he plays. He always seems to have a positive attitude and is more than willing to do his share. Budd has been a great help to me in my efforts to bring this book to print. His career in the newspaper business has helped beyond my expectations.

Budd loves a good story and of course a laugh or two from time to time. Laughter has been a very important part of our success as a group, and Budd does his share.

Figure 2 Budd with his Instruments.2009.

Mosquitoes and Black Flies. I think it would be appropriate to tell this story while I am working on Budd's chapter. This story is not about Budd but I know he will laugh when he reads it. For many years we have heard stories of large Mosquitoes, and of course the swarms of

Black flies. This story was passed along to me from an acquaintance of mine who had a daughter living in Yellowknife, NWT. On one of her phone calls to her mother she complained that, the Mosquitoes were terrible there. Her mother asked,"are they really big there?" Well, she said, " I am not saying they are that big but they land at the airport and walk into town".

Figure 3 Ron, Budd, Doug, and Nick At the Lodge.

I must tell you another story that is very closely related to Budd. We were on one of our visits to possum lodge and of course the meals were abundant. Following the evening meal we were relaxing and talking about the delicacy we had consumed. Now, Budd who could not be referred to as the Galloping Gourmet, was very interested in learning a few basic tips on how to prepare a basic meal. It was at this juncture that Al came to his rescue. He asked Budd if he ever heard of Popcorn Chicken the easy way. Budd was very interested in any easy way to prepare a meal, and was all ears, as he had not heard of such a meal.

Al went to great lengths to explain the whole process of preparing the chicken. This included cleaning and preparing the stuffing, along with the popping corn. He told him what temperature to set the oven, but did not give him the time it should cook. Budd was all ears at this point in time and mulled everything over in his astute mind. After he had thought a few moments he asked. "When I do all this and put it in the oven how long should it cook?" Al replied. "When the popcorn blows the ass off the chicken you will know it is cooked". Poor Budd was in shock for a few seconds and then joined the rest of us in laughter. We have often talked about this story, and every time we get another laugh.

Budd has contributed a lot to our group, and laughter has been a big part of the package. In troubled times we all need humour.

Chapter Fourteen: The Down Home Fiddlers

I thought it best that I dedicate a portion of this book to the above group. As I mentioned before, I feel it is one of the best in our area. I believe the main reason for this is the open concept of the group. We have by-laws that can be used to keep us on track, but for the most part each member can play the type of music they wish, and always on an equal basis.

We have a pool of co-ordinators that take turns running our weekly jam sessions. Everyone who wishes to play gets equal time at the mike. This process has proven to be very successful and we average over 30 members in attendance each night.

In addition to our regular weekly jam sessions we are called upon to play for several functions in the area and follow the same procedure for our leaders. Since we formed this group we have had several people take over the reins and put on a great show. Some of these people would never have dreamed of this a few years ago.

Our group was first formed in 1999 and has grown continuously since then. Most of us started out with the Metro Fiddlers but a parting of the ways, was needed. This is not meant to be a poor reflection on the other group, however we are much happier now and I dare say we are all much better players.

We have an elected executive and hold elections once a year. We welcome everyone who is interested to come along and join in the fun. Your level of playing skill will never be an issue. I have been a member from day one and I enjoy every event we have.

Like all groups there are times when we do not all agree but cooler heads prevail and we grow and become stronger. It is a great group of people that are also good friends. It is a pleasure to see so many people improve their skills on a continuing basis.

From top left to bottom right
Keith Filmore, Dance at Campbells, Edgil Dauphinee, Lorne Morash,
and Charley Rix (deceased)

From top left to bottom right. Susie Eisan, Bun Webber,(deceased)
and part of the Down Home Fiddlers at the Mall

Halloween Crazy.2009

The above pictures were taken at the Dialysis unit at the VG Hospital in Halifax. Note the special guests with The Down Home Fiddlers. The group performs at several functions throughout the region, and all on a voluntary basis. Each time they go out they have a different co-ordinator to direct them. This has been one of the biggest reasons for the absolute success of this group.

Following is a partial list of the Down Home Fiddlers.

Isabelle Conrad, Lorne Morash, Dianne Gazzola, Susan Eisan,

Helen Wiper, Betty Nieforth, Troy Nieforth, Gary Purdy ,

Virginia Walker, Nick Nicholson, Paul Aalders, Reta Cahil,

Doug Cooney, Mary Canning, Edgil Dauphinee, Diane Hicks,

Rick Fletcher, Anna Ellis, Ron Dares, Ida Leadley, Jack

Whiting, Marie Antle, Airen Antle, Keith Fillmore, Rhodes Killigrew,

Ken Hemeon, Bun Webber, Bud Humphries, Doreen Mallard,

Al McVicar, Don McVicar, Ron Hartley, Basil Miller, Betty-

Ann Miller, Sheila Mills, Robert Taylor, Vivian Taylor,

Charlie MacDonald, Carolyn Vaughan, Doug Morash, Budd

Gavel, Pat Meagher, Loretta MacDougall, Malcolm

MacDougall, Marg Thompson, Dennis Boudreau, Trish Otto

Chapter Fifteen: My Favourite Fiddlers.

I should point out that I favour local fiddlers. I think this is a good thing. It is like using Atlantic Canadian products. If we want to keep our local culture alive, we must support our local people. I have a lot of respect for all the fiddlers in Canada, but our local fiddlers are very talented as well, and yet, they are not always recognized. This is an easy problem to solve.

I thought I would mention a few of the fiddlers that I have met and have been influenced by their music. They are not in any particular order as I don't wish to categorise them, except for the very first one on the list. I have tried to cover a wide range of fiddlers that I know and I realize I have missed quite a few. The violin has become a very large part of my life, and these people have all helped me in trying to learn a few tunes.

Tara Lynn Touesnard. Who passed away in a tragic car accident in 1994. When people ask me, "who is the best fiddler you ever heard? It is so easy to answer. I know I will never live long enough to hear a better fiddler than Tara Lynn. I Don't expect to be proven wrong anytime soon. She had everything to offer. The beautiful music, right from her soul, the perfect presentation, a graceful style and a perfect smile that went on and on. There are a lot of fiddlers I like, but she was the very best.

Don Messer. He was, and still is a household name around the fiddling world. Anyone who plays the down-east style of music will certainly be playing a few of his tunes. I am one however, who preferred a few others. So I will be very candid about it. I think Don Messer had a great band, and his business- like attitude was successful, but I think the band made the music. Not to take anything from his playing ability, but his band was exciting. Don, I'm not so sure.

Lorimer Higgins One of the best dance fiddlers in Atlantic Canada. He grew up in Northern Nova Scotia, and now lives in Bridgewater. I have known this fellow for several years and I have had the opportunity to play with him several times. Each time it has been a pleasure. He has a special style and plays wonderful dance music. A few years back we met Lorimer and Shirley in Florida and played at several places there. He has recorded several albums and CDs and has composed thirty or more tunes. He must have a room full of trophies. In his early years he composed a tune called, The Tidal Bore Waltz which I believe was his first composition. This was a big hit, and was played on the local radio station in Truro. I think the tune was named via a contest at that radio station

.

Besides being a good fiddler he is also a great story teller. I will relate this one to you, that was told to me by Lorimer when he was spending his winters in Florida. He parked his motorhome in one of the RV Parks there. I believe it was Settlers Rest. He would get up early most mornings and go get a paper. The papers were in one of those metal boxes, and you deposited your money, pulled the door and got your paper. One morning early, he set out to do just that. He had to kneel down on one knee to put his money in and retrieve his paper. As he did so his sweater got caught in the door as he shut it. Now he had his paper, but his sweater was caught and he did not have any more change to get the door open again. He was concerned that someone would come along and find him stuck to the paper box. He worked around until he got himself out of the sweater and went back home to get some more money. You see, he had to go back and retrieve his sweater. What a thrill that would have been to get that on Video.

Cye Steele I have known Cye Steele for several years, and listened to his music long before that. He has been one of my favorite players, and has a very unique style, that has a way of making you listen when he plays. I met Cye for the first time when he was doing some deliveries for Canada Post in Truro, Nova Scotia. I also worked for Canada Post, I was working in the Marketing Branch at our Divisional office in Halifax. My work involved a lot of travel, and it was on one of these trips I met Cye. We talked about the fiddle of course as I was just starting to play. I have always tried to keep in touch and as a matter of fact, I saw him very recently in Wentworth Nova Scotia, at a dance. Unfortunately Cye is not in very good health, but he still has that magic touch. If I really wanted to copy any one fiddler, he would be the one. I have always had the view that each one of us should try to develop our own style, but he has a style I think I would like to copy. He has played for dances for over sixty years, has many recordings, played with Don Messer on Television, and the list goes on.

Ivan Hicks, New Brunswick. There is not enough one could say about this gentleman. He truly is the gentleman of the fiddle. Very talented and presents himself so well. As I have said before, presentation is a very important part of any show. Ivan is a prime example of that. He has many recordings and has travelled all over the country with his music. His wife Vivian is equally important and is just as impressive on stage. Ivan is a great Master of Ceremonies and is much in demand. A master at the fiddle and yet so unassuming. He has toured Canada and the United States, and was the driving force behind Fiddlers of The World, in Halifax in 1999

Dave Buckler, Truro, N.S. Dave is a fiddler who gives a lot of his time to music. He has a wide selection of good dance tunes and plays them very well. As we travel around the Province playing at special events, he is the one we see the most. He has judged for many contests, and has played at dances for many years.

Lawrence Buckler, Dartmouth, N.S. Lawrence is Dave's brother but unlike Dave we don't see him very often. We try to get him out to our Wednesday night group, but only once in a while will he show. Also a very talented fiddler and composer. He has a long list of great tunes. A great guy and we would love to see him more often.

Al McVicar, Dartmouth, N.S. Because I am very close to Al, being one of our band members, I tend to forget just how good he is. I don't know how many tunes the average fiddler knows, but Al probably knows close to a thousand tunes. Now, knowing that many is one thing, but to be able to re-call them is another. I would say that if you had a list of all the tunes he knew, and you picked them randomly, he could start a very high percentage immediately. Most people would not realize this as he is not one to brag about his abilities. In our area he has influenced more new fiddlers with his help than any other person I know.

Al is a very modest guy. Who plays from the heart, by ear. We frequently join him in chiding our friends that can not get away from the written notes. Al has been a tremendous help to me and I thank him for over half of the tunes I have learned.

Arden Hayman, Colchester County. I have known Arden for only a few years , but I am very impressed with his playing. I know he has played for several years, and has at least two CDs. Both great. When he plays one of his great reels, you will dance even if you have never danced before.

Willet Stevenson, Wentworth N.S. Another great fiddler who will keep your toes a-tapping. Willet is another that lends his help on many occasions. He too has judged at several contests.

Glendon Stevens, Collingwood N.S. One of the fiddlers from the era when old-time dances were held in every community. A great player and also a composer. A great friend of many people. Glendon is a good example of our traditional old-time fiddler.

Susie Eisan, Porters Lake N.S. She has a studio in Porters lake and teaches young and old. She has taken lessons from several people but I am sure she favours Gordon Stobbe, who I will mention next. The rising star, Susie is a great friend of mine and I have listened to her play from the time she started. She passed me in a few lessons. She has such a great talent. She loves to play and it shows when she is on stage. She is also one of the best teachers in our area. Because of my business I see several of her students and they all love her. We are very fortunate to have her teaching and helping so many new fiddlers, young and old. I once told Susie she was as close to Tara Lynn Touesnard as I had ever heard. She did not remember Tara Lynn, but I hope she knows what a compliment that was.

Gordon Stobbe, Seaforth N.S. Gordon impressed me from day one. Not just the fact that he is good, but that he has so many styles. Gordon hosted **Up Home Tonight** a few years back, and has been teaching here for several years. He has taught at several workshops all across this country and is much in demand. I have attended many fiddle workshops over the past several years, and his is by far the best. He makes everything so practical and so much fun. Gordon plays a variety of music and perhaps not all will turn you on, but he is the most capable fiddler in our area. Give him a style you like to hear and he will play it.

John Afton Maclellan, This gentleman, the left- handed fiddler, was once on Thrill of a Lifetime playing a genuine Stradivarius. He is a great gentleman and we had the pleasure of playing at his 100 Birthday party in Nine Mile River April 3rd 2008. And his 101st birthday in 2009. Again for his 102nd. April 2010.

Figure 1 John Afton with his certificate of appreciation.

Figure 2 Owen's 65th Birthday, at the Bedford Legion He is in the centre.

Owen Davis, A true Friend. This gentleman is not a fiddle player, but represents the people who loves to listen and dance to our music. I first met Owen when I was associated with the Maritime Fiddle Festival. He had been a sponsor for the Lower Sackville fiddle contest, and since it had shut down, I was told to contact him. This was to be a meeting that never ended. We seemed to hit it off well together from day one. I think because we were both from the old school, where you worked hard at what you had to do, and you appreciated what you had.

We keep in touch, mainly to keep him informed of our up-coming dances, and to talk about antiques, auctions, cars and trucks. And to tell a few stories. We sometimes refer to him as the tractor man, because of his large collection of International tractors. He loves to sing and we encourage him to take part every chance we get. It is always a pleasure to hear from him from time to time and when we talk, there is always a lot of laughter. You never know where he could be at any given time. He might be in Manitoba looking at an old tractor or he might be flying over the Grand Canyon. I know for sure he loves to dance, and we love to see him there to dance. Good friends are treasures and he is a treasure. We can thank Owen for more support to Old-time fiddling than he would readily admit.

Donald Isenor, Milford N.S. The first time I heard this man play I was totally impressed with his style. I have had the opportunity to play with him on several occasions since and I am still impressed. He is a very modest person and I am sure he is not aware of his unique style. I attended a concert a few years ago where there were a few top notch fiddlers. Donald was there with his daughter Kimberley, and played a couple of tunes. When we were leaving a friend of mine said to me, " you can bring fiddlers from all over the world, but I still like Donald Isnor." I shared those feelings. There is something very special about most of our older fiddlers. It is like a language dialect of different areas. Each one has a special style depending on the area or their source of music. What a shame this is being eroded.

Kimberly Holmes Isenor. What a treat it is to hear her play the fiddle. She is without a doubt one of the best pianists in this area and is known all over Canada for her accomplishments, but a lot of people don't know how well she plays the fiddle. There is such a gentle sweetness about her playing. She is also one of the best known fiddle teachers in our area. Thanks to her efforts there are countless numbers of new fiddlers in Nova Scotia.

Mel MacPhee. This man has been playing for most of his life and still entertains many, many people. I first met him in the early 50's when he played for the dances in Upper Musquodoboit. What a great person he is and always has a laugh or two every time you see him. Like most of my favourites he is from the old school, simple and sweet. It is always a pleasure to play with this gentleman.

.

Bernard Rogers. Bernard is no longer with us, and may not have been as well known as most, but he was a very special fiddler. Born in the Musquodoboit Valley and spending most of his years there, along with the Stewiacke Valley. He was best known for his dance music. We had an opportunity to play with him on a few occasions. Unfortunately he passed away a few years ago. I remember playing with him one night when his Arthritis was so bad he could only use two fingers on the violin. Even then he could play as good as the best.

Jamie Durning, Jamie plays the fiddle much better than he lets on, but that is not why I include him with the rest. Jamie has a special connection to fiddle music. He remembers more tunes and their composers than anyone else I know. Besides this, he and his wife Liz devote as much time to the preservation of, down-east music than anyone else in this Province. Thank you Jamie and Liz for all your efforts.

Ervin MacCoul. This gentleman has also left us but he was one of the people who gave me the encouragement to keep playing. When I met him, he lived in Antigonish, Nova Scotia. Vivian and I would go to Barney's River to visit her relatives Oak and Mae Dean. They had a son Bobby who played a mean guitar and Ervin would come down from Antigonish to join the fun. I was just learning a few tunes at the time and Ervin would always encourage me to join in. We became great friends and I will always remember those days and the fun we had. He had a long list of tunes he played and never read a note.

David Perrin. David was a special fiddling friend of mine. He lost his life in a tractor accident several years ago. He was very instrumental in helping me with my fiddle. He gave me an opportunity to see the real fun in playing. He was not your high end performer, but he had an exceptional attitude towards enjoying while you learn. I have never forgotten the many laughs we had while learning new tunes. He struck me as a man who lived life the way it should be lived. He always had time for others. Deadlines did not appear to be part of his lifestyle. He worked hard when he had to but always found time for the little things in life.

This is a short story about Dave and his priorities. Vivian and I were on our way to visit her father and mother, who lived in Dean, a quiet little Village in Halifax County. Dave owned a farm just across the road from Vivian's parents. Quite frequently we would invite him and his wife down when we were there, for a tune or two.

On this occasion Dave was out in the field bailing hay. When we arrived, it was early evening and I knew he had another two hours of sunlight before he would have to quit work. I suggested we let his wife Frances know we were there and invite them down later. When we called, Frances sent one of the children out to the field to give him the message. I could see the young boy run out to him, but of course I could not hear the message. In an instant Dave left the tractor and bailer and headed for the house. I could tell right away, that playing the fiddle was far more important to him at that moment than bailing hay. Twenty minutes later he was showered, and down playing his fiddle with us.

We would get together many more times after that and every time there would be lots of laughter. It was a very sad time when he passed away and we all felt the pain. We try to keep in touch with his family and we have watched the children grow to be adults with families of their own.

Kirk Logan. Kirk was one of the best fiddlers in the province, and he happened to live near my father's home in Upper Musquodoboit. In my early teens, Kirk was my barber. He had a little shop beside his house and it was a great place to hang out even when you did not need a haircut. It was not until later years that I realized what a good fiddler he was. He played for dances in Elderbank Nova Scotia, for quite a long time and then began a long string of Fiddle Contests where he took many prizes My wife Vivian accompanied him on the piano on several occasions.

I had an opportunity to play with him at Upper Musquodoboit later on and was overwhelmed by his ability. It was at this dance that I learned my first lesson on playing what the people want to hear. He had finished a tune, and a lady came up and asked him to play Maple Sugar. He said, " I can't play that unless I have a bucket to barf in when I am finished." The lady laughed. He laughed, but I didn't. From that day on I decided I would always try to play what the people wanted to hear.

Marshall Bayers. Marshall is now over ninety years of age and lives in Musquodoboit Harbour. When I first met him he had joined us at Lawrencetown, Nova Scotia for one of our dances. He had such a unique, and sweet sound. I remember listening to the tunes he played and just being captured by his style. You could go to a dozen contests anywhere in the country and not see anything like it. Would he win a prize at a contest? Probably not, but he would sure grab the attention of everyone in the audience.

Kenny Murphy. This fellow was a man I will never forget. He died a few years back, however I had many chances to meet with Kenny. I first met him at the Maritime Fiddle Festival in Dartmouth Nova Scotia. He was always a hit at this event and looked forward to attending every year. During one of my many trips to hunt for old fiddles, I ran across Kenny who just happened to be staying with the person I was going to see. From that day on he would call me at least once a month and often more frequently. As soon as he found out I restored violins he was my friend for life. Later on he moved to a Home for Special Care in Dartmouth and I dropped in to see him as often as I could.

One day I visited him at his request. He had dropped his rosin and broke it in several pieces. This was a ploy of his to get me to go see him. I was quite taken by this man and a little curious about him as well. Since I had not met him in his early years, I asked him what he did for a living. He replied, " I avoided work most of my life. I did have a job during the Second World War It lasted three days." He went on to explain that he had survived quite well all his life without working. I was surprised to hear this but I did not question him any further. I thought about his working life later and realized he seemed to be quite content now in this home and had most of the comforts we all look for. Kenny was not one of the best fiddlers I ever met but he was a very interesting person, and he made an impression on a lot of people.

Harold Tibbitts. Harold lives in Bedford Nova Scotia. I am not sure he is playing now. I first met Harold when he was playing with the Friday Night Fiddlers. This was a small group that played together for several years in the Halifax Dartmouth area. I don't think I would be out of line if I said he was the lead fiddler in that group. I don't know if they played for many dances but they sure did get around to a lot of other events. Harold had a style that was unlike any other fiddler I have known. I suppose some teachers would frown on his technique, but when they heard him play they would sure appreciate his music.

Harold Warmen. Harold was another member of the Friday Night Fiddlers, and a good fiddler. I did not get to know him well before he passed away, but he was a very good fiddler and a nice man. I will always remember how well he played the Cheticamp Reel.

Art Gray. Art was from Sambro Nova Scotia. He was one of a kind. He could build a fiddle in about two weeks and play it like it was a genuine Stradivarius. I visited his workshop on a couple of occasions to see the tools he used to make his violins. They were very limited. He was once disqualified from a fiddle contest because he did not hold the fiddle under his chin. What a farce that was. That man was a very soft and gentle player, and his music was so pleasing to the ear. He was a crowd pleaser from a way back. He passed away several years ago, but he has left us with many memories.

Jack Sibley. Jack and I have been friends for many years. We went to High School together however we lived about 25 miles apart. So we did not get to see each other except for school. It was several years later when I became interested in the fiddle, that we renewed friendships. Jack is a very good old time fiddler. He is a very modest player, and will try to keep in the background. He has been teaching fiddle classes in Truro, Nova Scotia, for several years and has become one of the finest teachers we have. I have had the good fortune to attend several of his closing concerts in the spring, and to see the respect his students show for him, is a tribute to his style. He is a lover of the Don Messer style of music and it shows in his students.

Jack is also a very good Master of Ceremonies and can be seen at many functions. I do a little of this too, so it is always fun to watch Jack, and learn from him. We often have fun taking shots at one another, when we are together. The man has integrity written all over him. There are very few people in this area that have done as much to help preserve our fiddling heritage.

There is one fiddler that I heard, but never did remember his name. My wife and I were attending a Fiddle contest in Pictou Nova Scotia about twenty years ago. Along towards the end of the show, and I think it would have been the open category, a gentleman walked out on stage to play, with a chair. He sat down and played his three tunes, very well. The people were dancing in several parts of the arena as he played. When he finished the crowd came to their feet with loud applause. When the judges gave their final decision, this man was not among the top three or four. I felt so sad for this man and wondered how he must have felt. He was certainly recognized by the audience, but not the judges. I don't want to give anyone the impression that I think our judges are incompetent. I do think however that they have to step outside the box and listen to the audience. If it were not for the audience where would we be. This is true whenever and wherever we play. The audience is very important wether it be two hundred people or just one. Like I said, I do not remember the man's name but if I did he would sure be on my list.

All of the people I have selected are part of a group that have stood out in my mind. Some have left us but most remain to continue doing what they do so well. A few of these people have done very well at contests across canada, and have gained tremendous recognition. The majority of these people however, are just ordinary fiddle players who love to play and help others. I like a player who tries just as hard when he or she is playing for a few Seniors at a Home for Special Care, as they do when they are playing for a large crowd of people.

I am always equally impressed with how they present themselves, as well as the musical ability they have. I know a few fiddlers who would prefer to play at home for their own enjoyment. This is fine if that is what they really want to do. However, musical talent, like any other talent should be shared It is a gift, share it in a modest and pleasing manor and be we rewarded.

Figure 3 Our very good friend Bobby Watters from Scotsburn Nova Scotia. He is also a good fiddler.

Chapter Sixteen: Linda Gail Brown Rix Born June 1st 1945
In Caribou Gold Mines, Halifax County Nova Scotia.

Music is well said to be the speech of Angels. Thomas Carlyle.

Figure 1 Linda with her new Violin.

Linda's first desire to get involved in music was in grade 7 (1957) when she received a violin from her parents. She took lessons for several months before moving to Dartmouth with her family Twenty two years later she took ukulele lessons and joined an adult ensemble under the direction of Chalmers Doane.

She took part in many performances including several in Hawaii in 1988. In 1989 Linda learned to play the upright bass, starting with Bluegrass music. A couple of years later she joined the Chebucto Big Band, with whom she played for 15 years at numerous functions including the Jazz Festival every summer. In 1997 Linda had the honour of playing bass in The Music Man, at the Rebecca Cohn with the Nova Scotia Drama league.

In recent years Linda has played with the Easy Tones, and continues to play with The Dartmouth Concert Band, Timeless (an eight piece swing band), The Last Chance Band and the Country Stompers (Old-time dance bands).

This past year Linda has had the pleasure of playing with the Christian Academy, in The Fiddler on the Roof. Linda enjoys playing all kinds of music. This portion of Linda's profile was written by her daughter.

Linda has always had an open invitation to play with The Last Chance Band even though she has never become a full time member. With her hectic schedule, it is difficult for her to be with us on a frequent basis. We do however, welcome her when she can, as she adds so much to our music. She is very talented and is certainly a lively performer. Nick, our regular bass player moves to the guitar when Linda is with us. Nick is an excellent bass player as well as a guitar player and the two of them make our music so much better.

When Linda joins our group there is always that little extra spark, and I am sure it shows in our audience. People who have that little added touch can take any music to a higher level.

I grew up in the same area as Linda, however I did not know her well, as she is younger than I. Linda and her two sisters, Veida, and Karen, both attended Musquodoboit Rural High. We see them and their mother, Marion at a lot of our dances. Linda, along with her mother and sisters are excellent dancers. Linda often takes a break from her playing to go down on the dance floor to have a whirl. There are times when I am sure it is hard for her to decide which she would rather do. She is always cheerful and willing to play any tunes we select. I believe that attitude plays a very strong part in the success of any musician and she is certainly blessed with the right attitude.

Linda lost her husband Gary, in September 2007 in a tragic accident and has had a trying adjustment to unfortunate circumstances. We all tried to be a comfort to her and support her as much as possible. One can only try to imagine how hard it must have been for her. She keeps herself very busy and her family are there for her. I know for sure The last Chance Band were all very glad to see her back playing again.

She joins us quite often when we go to Upper Musquodoboit, as that area was her original home. It is like home to all of the band now, as we have developed so many friends there. Two of the main things we look for when we play are, a good floor and good acoustics. This dance hall has both. Add to that a friendly crowd and you have an excellent mix.
From the very first time she played with us we were delighted to have her join us. As long as we play, she will always be a welcome addition. When our friends know Linda is going to play, there are more of them come out. This is a great tribute to Linda, and her playing.

Figure 2 Linda at her beautiful home in
Minesville, Nova Scotia. She is a busy lady
and adds new life wherever she plays.

The pictures on the following page were taken recently at a
birthday party for John Afton McLellan in Elmsdale.Nova Scotia.He
was one hundred and two years old Saturday April 3rd. There were
over forty fiddlers and several other musicians gathered there along
with many friends. These five gentlemen played together and
sounded great. Their total age at the time was 460 years. Each one
has a unique style and showed it for this event. Since Linda is the
youngest to play in our group I decided to add these gentlemen to
her profile.

Figure 4 Don Iesnor 84

Figure 7 Lew Garby 88

Figure 6 John Afton McLellan 102

Figure 5 Lloyd Tattrie 97

Figure 8 Mel MacPhee 89

Each of these gentlemen have played for many dances, and other events for many years. Just try to imagine the stories they could tell.

Chapter Seventeen: Robert Corey Taylor

Born June 5th 1938 at Stewart Hill, Upper Musquodoboit
Nova Scotia.
The second youngest of eight Children.

All of my school training was received in the Musquodoboit
Valley. During my last year of high school I decided I wanted to join the
RCMP. I was interviewed and passed the written exam, but due to my
lack of weight I was turned down. They should see me now. I am not
sure that I would have made a good policeman, however I was willing
to try. I decided later that year I would follow the path of so many Nova
Scotians and head for Toronto. I am not saying this was a good idea but
it was a great experience for me, the youngster from the country. At that
time finding a job was very easy, especially if you were from the
Maritimes. You see, we were used to hard work and had a better
reputation of work ethic than most at that time.

After a few months I returned and began working for the Bank
of Nova Scotia in Truro, Nova Scotia. After just two years I left the
bank, got married, and went back to Toronto. Stayed again for six
months, and then my wife and I came back home to stay. I joined
Canada Post in 1960, and remained there for thirty three years. As I look
back I realize this was a good move for me. The Corporation was very
good for me and I was able to further my
knowledge and spend the last twenty years
in sales and marketing, at the divisional
office in Halifax. The highlight of my postal
career was in Ottawa where I trained other
employees on personal sales techniques.
This training gave me countless advantages
after I retired.

In 1991 I opened a Stringed
Instrument business in my home, called
Fiddle Sticks Instruments. After eighteen
years I am still at it.

I am the proud father of three
wonderful sons, who are married. There are
also four granddaughters.

Figure 1 Rob on
Stewart Hill1940

During the mid eighties I decided to learn the Violin. This is when my life started to take a giant turn. Music has had a tremendous impact on my life. Some of the best friends I have, I met through music.

As I look back over my early years, I have very fond memories, even though they were hard times. I remember being at a family reunion several years ago and listening to my brother Keith talking to one of our cousins. This particular cousin felt he was just a little better than most. He said, "You folks were real poor when you were young." My brother replied, "Yes but we did not know it at the time." I have often thought about this and my brother was right. Most of us in that area were from poor times and poor families, but we did very well with what we had. We lived in normal conditions for that time, and were thankful.

I am not suggesting that our families today should go back to this, but I do believe hard times build character. When I first started to school, my brothers and sisters went with me, however I got out of school earlier and had to walk home by myself. It was over a mile and that was with the short cuts through the pastures. In winter I would be in snow up to my waist for a lot of this travel. I will never forget that experience. I wore riding britches, and lumberman's rubbers. To those of you old enough to remember you will certainly know what happened when you walked in deep snow. When your feet went down, the snow went up your leg. When your feet came up the snow went in your boots. I could go on but I think you get the drift, if you'll pardon the pun.

At the time there were trying times, but I am glad I had the experience. I would not trade those times for school buses, or snow days, like we have today. Oh yes, I must tell you. At that point in my life I whistled all the time, mostly old-time music. You see I had the bug even then. If you ever meet any of my siblings just ask them. They used to tell me to get out of their sight, or go outside and whistle. I think they were jealous.

My brother Mac used to whistle, but only if he was in the dark. I guess he thought it would scare off all forms of danger. On that point he was right. His whistling would scare anything. He passed away a few years ago, and I still miss him very much. He was my closest brother, in age and was my mentor in many ways.

I must tell you about another member of my family. Frances is my oldest sister. When my mother passed away Frances would have been about seventeen. Prior to this when my mother was sick, Frances became a housekeeper and a mother to me. She went to school and did lots of household chores. I remember one year in particular that stands out in my memory. She had picked berries and made preserves for the winter months. She also made pickles and jams and jelly. These were all placed on old shelves in the basement. One or two of the shelves gave out and most of her bottles were broken. I was quite young at the time but I never forgot how sorry I was. It was not only the loss of the bottles, but all the hard work my sister went through. She had her eighty third birthday in 2009, and she is still a hard worker and a splendid Mom. Not only to her little brother but to her own family of seven.

Several years ago I had a dream of playing for an audience. I just wanted to make people happy. Music has given me that opportunity. I know I will never reach stardom, that was never my wish. Many times when we play, I look out at our dancers or our listening audience and I see a radiance that we created. We can touch people in a very special way. That is a good feeling. Now, when I think of those treks through the snow drifts, I realize that every step was worth it.

I had several reasons for writing this book, but I think the main reason was to thank all of the wonderful people who came out to listen and to dance to our music. You have warmed the hearts of everyone in our band. I wanted to find a way to pass on a very special message to all who would read and listen. Music is the lifeblood of all of us. It is great to be able to play but when people listen and enjoy, it takes on a whole new meaning. Truly, the audience makes it all worthwhile. You don't have to be the best in order to please your audience. Do your best and be proud of the level you are at. Be humble and let your mind go, beyond the music.

Thanks to all of our friends for supporting us, and following us from gig to gig. It has been a   pleasure to be able to relate a few stories and I hope you will enjoy. Special thanks to all the members of our band for helping put this book together.

While I was in the rather long process of writing this book, I lost two of my best friends. Herman KacKeen, and Keith MacLennan. I did manage to finish Herman's chapter before he passed away. I delivered it to him just before he died. I was not able to do this for Keith. There were times when I did not think I would ever finish the task, but they became my inspiration. They are both gone now but they still walk with me.

Figure 2   Rob, Summer 2008

As we get older I think we learn to cherish the happy moments even more. I have, along with the rest in our band, been able to bring happiness to a lot of our very good friends. This has been a joy for me too. I have always wanted to end each day knowing I did something good for my family and brought a little comfort to my friends.

I remember reading a poem called Slow Dance. I would like to pass it along to you as it is so true. This was written by a young girl who was terminally ill. It is presented to you in her exact words.

Have you ever watched kids on a merry-go-round?
Or listened to the rain slapping on the ground?
Followed a butterfly's erratic flight?

Or gazed at the sun into the fading night?
You better slow down.
Don't dance so fast. Time is short. The music won't last.

Do you run through each day on the fly? When you ask, how are you,
do you hear the reply? When day is done, do you lie in your bed,
with your next hundred chores running through your head?

*You'd better slow down. Don't dance so fast. Time is short.
The music won't last.*

*Ever told your child, we'll do it tomorrow? And in your haste
not see their sorrow?*

*Ever lost touch. Let a good friendship die, cause you never
had time to call and say Hi?*

*You'd better slow down. Don't dance so fast. Time is short.
The music won't last.*

*When you run so fast to get somewhere, you miss half the fun
of getting there.*

*When you worry and hurry through your day, it is like an
unopened gift Thrown away.*

*Life is not a race. Take it slower. Hear the music
Before the music is over.*

     I hope this book has touched the hearts of at least a few.
It has been a learning experience for me and a lot of fun as well.
As you pass through your life do yourself a big favour.
Whatever you are doing please take time to stop and smell the
Roses.

     So many times in our lives we plan to do things with the
best intentions, but because we are in such a rush we forget and
move on. Life is not a race. Take your time and enjoy the
journey.

Figure 3 My Twins Both 1952 Models. My pride and Joy.

The Chevy on the left I purchased when my good friend Keith was with me. The Pontiac on the right belonged to Keith. I purchased it from his wife and daughter after he died.

Chapter 18 The Conclusion

After many months of deciding what to write, and how to put it all together, I find myself nearing the end of a very rewarding experience. I think it was about four years ago the idea first crossed my mind. I wanted to leave something behind that would give people some idea of how a group like The Last Chance Band became successful and touched the hearts of many people. I realize there are a lot more groups out there who have gained more in a monetary way, but that was never our objective. Money was never in our plans. You can not put a price tag on the things we have done together. From day one our objective was to play for dances and make people happy. We have been very successful at that, and proud of our accomplishments.

We have played for countless anniversaries, birthday parties, and dances galore. At this point in time we do not know how much longer we will continue, but not one of us would change a thing we have done so far.

I have strayed from the subject a few times in other chapters, and talked more about my own personal life. I did this for two reasons. The first reason was to give the readers a view of a few things that happened in my past. The second was to make a comparison of the lives of all of us. We all grew up at the same time and our lives were quite similar. There is no doubt that is one of the reasons we get along well together. We have had times when things did not go real smooth, but nothing that would be worth printing. I have always been considered the Boss, and I take this very kindly. Almost every decision we make is on a consensus basis so that everyone has their say. I can't think of a better way and we have proven that it works.

When more than one person is playing, you have a team. In order to be successful everyone must be a team member. Each one has a part to play and they do so without trying to take over the show. I have known several groups in our area who had the skill levels to succeed but just could not develop the cooperative spirit that was needed. They are history now. We are very fortunate that we had the ability to work as a team and above all else listen to our audience. When our Thursday night practice comes around we hash over previous events and look for the

123

strong and the weak points. We discuss new tunes and schedule the old ones that people never get tired of. It is a constant exercise to keep a few new tunes on our list. When we try a new tune we ask our audience for their input. If they are not overly happy we would not likely play it again. There are other times when we get asked to play tunes that we are tired of. We will still play these tunes however as that is what people want.

In another chapter I mentioned a few of the crazy things we have done. I should also give you an idea of a few of the things that we did that gave us a great sense of giving. From the very first time we played, we have been giving donations to charities. I am not sure of the exact amount, but I would say it would be in the vicinity of $50,000. All of this would have been distributed in the local area. We are very proud of this, yet we have never dwelled on the subject as there was never any need. I just feel it is a good time to mention this, as we have always played for the joy of playing.

Most of the groups I know, do the same thing. There are many who get paid a small amount, but I am not aware of any that are getting rich. They all give a lot of their time to help others. Music is a wonderful thing, and when you can use it to help others it is even better.

Finding a way to express the gratitude we feel towards all of our loyal followers is very difficult. There are so many people to name and not enough explanatory terms to cover our thoughts. The friends we have made and the good times we have had, are all part of, and a result of our Music. Over the years we have travelled many miles to play, and experienced all kinds of driving conditions, only to find that several others travelled the same distance just to hear our music. When people travel over 50 miles each way on a cold winter night, to dance to our music, we know we are doing something right. I am sure that will remain in our hearts as long as we live.

I personally believe I, along with every member of our band have made a mark, and I hope this book will give others the incentive to do the same. People who donate their time for others, (especially musical entertainment,) are a special breed and deserve a lot of credit.

I would like to pass on a message to all musicians. Regardless of your playing ability, be it professional or just a beginner, find time to help others. The rewards far out weigh the effort. I know a lot of people who play musical instruments who do not have the courage to play out side of their own safety zone. I have encouraged several to step out and be proud of their ability, and found it very rewarding. The majority of people listening, are not judgmental. They are in fact quite the opposite.

Music is a wonderful treasure. We should play, listen, and enjoy every minute. Some people love to play, others love to listen. Don't miss a chance to give the listeners an opportunity to hear, regardless of your ability.

The following statistics are reasonably accurate and will give some indication as to the number of times we have played together. This information is based on activities over a 16 year period.

Practise nights	700
Jam Sessions	600
Dances	520
Playing for Seniors	500
Anniversaries	50
Concerts etc.	35
Total	2405

In addition to these events we found time to produce four tapes and two cd's. All of this was done because we wanted to have fun and create enjoyment for others.

I don't want to dwell on the things we have done but I would like to mention one other thing that puts things in perspective. Recently we took part in a fund raiser for a local Home for Special Care. We helped raise over a $1000.00. This money was used to give the residents an opportunity to enjoy a few small pleasures they would not get under normal circumstances. A trip to a special show and a feed of fresh Lobster, just to mention a few. When we think how good these people must feel when someone cares enough to go that extra step for them is very rewarding. We did not do this on our own, we just helped make it possible.

I believe everyone of us should take that extra step to help improve the quality of life for others. You might be surprised how easy it is and in turn feel the genuine rewards.

When it comes to musical groups, we are just one grain of sand on a mile long beach. Should you walk that beach sometime, I hope you notice us and remember the good times.

Below you will see a few of the many positive comments made about our dances.

To the Last Chance Band. We love hanging!! out with you. Have enjoyed your great music and have had lots of fun.   Betty Ann & Basil.

Thanks for all the good times we had at all the dances. I hope you all play for a good many years. Love   Cookie.

Roses are red, Violets are blue. I've sure enjoyed Dancing to you. Love Audrey.

We have enjoyed you and your music so very, very much. Good music, good friends, good times.   Laurie & Betty.

So glad I came to the dance that first time. Now I don't ever want to stop.   Karen.

We were concerned that growing old would be dull and boring, but you guys have given us a new lease on life. Thank you for all the pleasure you have given and may you live to see five score and ten.   Muriel & Bill

Can't thank you enough for the way the Last Chance Band has enriched our life. Our very best wishes to each and everyone of you.   Bill & Nancy.

You guys and Vivian are all such great people. You are so generous with your talent and we sure appreciate you. You are the greatest kind of

friends. Thank you so much for sharing your talent and time. Love to all of you.   Doreen Alex & Barb .